What people are saving about

Zeitgeist N

From Trump's backward-looking promise great again" to the hipster's fondness for a pre-industrial age of craft, nostalgia saturates our world. Gandini's book is a remarkable and insightful guide to this phenomenon, laying out the deep roots of its origins and setting out the contours of its limits.
Nick Srnicek, co-author of *Inventing the Future: Postcapitalism and a World Without Work*

Nostalgia has become a pivotal driver in politics, work and consumption, but the role it plays is complex. This book is the most insightful and accessible treatment of this important topic that I have read. A key text for understanding contemporary modernity.
Giana M. Eckhardt, Professor of Marketing, Royal Holloway, University of London

An essential map for anyone seeking to navigate a time that is thoroughly out of joint. Gandini steers us through the rear-view fantasies of contemporary populist politics, the retro-artisanal imaginaries of consumption and work in the Hipster economy, and the spectre of Marx animating techno-utopian dreams of a fully-automated luxury communism. The result is enlightening and unsettling in equal measures.
Chris Land, Professor of Work and Organization, Anglia Ruskin University

Agree or disagree with its rangy, punchy takes spanning Brexit, hipsterdom, Trump, postcapitalism and the world of work,

Gandini's page-turner is a pacey and accessible primer to some of the central cultural, political and economic dynamics of our time and the possible futures that lie ahead.

Frederick Harry Pitts, Lecturer in Management, University of Bristol and co-editor of *Futures of Work*

Zeitgeist Nostalgia

On populism, work and
the "good life"

Zeitgeist Nostalgia

On populism, work and
the "good life"

Alessandro Gandini

Winchester, UK
Washington, USA

JOHN HUNT PUBLISHING

First published by Zero Books, 2020
Zero Books is an imprint of John Hunt Publishing Ltd., No. 3 East St., Alresford,
Hampshire SO24 9EE, UK
office@jhpbooks.com
www.johnhuntpublishing.com
www.zero-books.net

For distributor details and how to order please visit the 'Ordering' section on our website.

Text copyright: Alessandro Gandini 2019

ISBN: 978 1 78904 447 8
978 1 78904 448 5 (ebook)
Library of Congress Control Number: 2019950473

A CIP catalogue record for this book is available from the British Library.

Design: Stuart Davies

UK: Printed and bound by CPI Group (UK) Ltd, Croydon, CR0 4YY
US: Printed and bound by Thomson-Shore, 7300 West Joy Road, Dexter, MI 48130

We operate a distinctive and ethical publishing philosophy in
all areas of our business, from our global network of authors to
production and worldwide distribution.

Contents

Acknowledgments

Part of the reason why you can read this book is because, two summers before its publication, instead of discouraging me Adam Arvidsson pushed me beyond my comfort zone to turn my reflections on nostalgia into a book for all to read. I am deeply grateful for his continuing guidance and inspiration.

I am also very much indebted and grateful to all those who took the time to read, discuss, comment and engage with earlier drafts of this work, particularly: Massimo Airoldi, Tiziano Bonini, Carolina Bandinelli, Alberto Cossu, Giana Eckhardt, Alessandro Caliandro, and my PhD students Silvia Semenzin, Lucia Bainotti, Giulia Giorgi and Ilir Rama, who all had to deal with my passionate elaborations (i.e., rants) about nostalgia at some point. Their comments, thoughts and reactions made this book a better one. The mistakes you will find in it, instead, are all mine.

Sparse thanks also go to my old and new colleagues at King's College London, particularly Nick Srnicek, Jennifer Pybus, Jonathan Gray, Rebecca Saunders and Sophie Bishop, and the University of Milan, particularly Luisa Leonini and Lisa Dorigatti, who variously supported me throughout this journey, sometimes simply by lending their ears to listen. Huge thanks also to Erica and Luca, who gave me food for thought every time we discussed about nostalgia. Above all, thanks to Francesca, who has patiently stuck with me despite I haven't really talked about much else over the last 2 years.

1. Nostalgia

My soul slides away
But don't look back in anger
I heard you say
Oasis, Don't Look Back in Anger

23 June 2016, some time around midnight, UK time.

As the Brexit vote coverage unfolds, news breaks that Sunderland, known as Britain's Ohio, a key battleground to understand where the political wind blows, voted to Leave by a significant margin. I go to bed but can't sleep well. At 6am, nervous, I pick up the tablet from my bedside. Leave won. While deep down I knew this was bound to happen, as the sentiment around the country was quite clear in the days prior to the referendum, the official results come as a big shock. I will never forget the thick silence on the streets of London the following day, with people almost apologetically refraining from making eye contact with one another. The sense was that we had just witnessed a turning point, without knowing what's around the corner.

* * *

8 November 2016, some time around midnight, UK time.

MSNBC polling commentator Steve Kornacki looks surprised. Something unexpected is taking place. Republican voter turnout in key states is reported to be significantly high. Florida, then Ohio. Pennsylvania, then Wisconsin. Then Michigan, too close to call. And finally, it dawns: Donald Trump, the man who some say never wanted to be President, has become President of the United States of America. Surprise, bewilderment and outrage in the Western world.

* * *

Soon after the Brexit and Trump votes, a flood of articles on why and how these two events happened occupied the pages of newspapers and magazines, while hours were spent on radio and television networks to unpack their implications. Since then, mountains of academic work have been produced, and countless debates held. Yet many questions still remain unanswered. This book asks one in particular: what if Brexit and the Trump election represent some kind of pivotal moment, being the most visible signs of a societal transition from one state of things to another?

Brexit and the Trump election are, at their core, a reaction to a decade of economic austerity following the 2007-08 financial crash, and a consequence of the inability of the West to imagine a future *beyond* it. As Mark Fisher famously noted, "it is easier to imagine the end of the world than the end of capitalism."[1] In the aftermath of a catastrophic economic crisis, Brexit and Trump offered instead an easy solution – to look *back*. Their slogans embody a populist fantasy of nostalgia, to "take back control" and "make America Great Again," that successfully flirted with the feelings of disenchantment, anger, anxiety and fear experienced in the Western world, particularly by those who have been hit the hardest by the economic downturn. Both the Leave and Trump campaigns promised a return to the world before the crisis, a simpler world made of nation-states, hard borders and a largely white, ethnically homogeneous, heterosexual and patriarchal society. Brexit and Trump are, in other words, the most conspicuous manifestations of the cultural zeitgeist of the start of the twenty-first century: nostalgia.

* * *

We live in an age of nostalgia: as French sociologist Edgar Morin would say, nostalgia represents the *spirit of the time* at the start of the twenty-first century.[2] A sentiment of nostalgia seems to pervade Western society, in politics and in popular culture, after more than 10 years of economic downturn and in the midst of a phase of technological transformation that has impacted processes of production, consumption and socialization to a largely unprecedented extent. But what is this nostalgia *about*, exactly? This book aims to show that this twenty-first century nostalgia is the somewhat natural reaction by Western society to the collapse of the societal model that affirmed in the twentieth century after World War II, built upon work as the bedrock of social cohesion and the conduit to living a "good life." The demise of a society constructed around work, and the difficulty to imagine an alternative to it, are a disorienting perspective for large parts of the Western populations. Nostalgia offers a relief to this anxiety and a comforting refuge from a world that, for many, has changed too much, too fast. But how did we get here?

The end of the "long twentieth century"

The twentieth century occupies a peculiar place in the history of society. Social historian Giovanni Arrighi describes it as the "long" twentieth century, being the latest in a series of "cycles of accumulation" that characterize the unfolding of modern capitalism since the Middle Ages. Each cycle of accumulation in Arrighi's model is dominated by a major player that occupies a hegemonic role in each phase, before being replaced by another one. From the Genoese domination of the 1300s, through a Dutch and then a British leadership into the 1800s, the cyclical evolution of capitalism reached the "long" twentieth century – the American century. This, for Arrighi, begins around 1870, in coincidence with the Second Industrial Revolution, and is marked by the affirmation of the United States of America as the leading economic and political player of modernity.[3]

Yet, compared to other cycles of accumulation there is one further aspect that peculiarly connotes the "long" twentieth century. In the period that followed World War II, Western society experienced an unprecedented phase of flourishing. Commonly described as an economic boom, an economic miracle or, perhaps more appropriately, the Golden Age of Capitalism,[4] this consisted in a period of sustained economic growth that extended across a variety of countries, starting obviously with the war winners but also including the quickly-westernizing, post-atomic Japan. This period of economic flourishing is usually understood to begin around 1950 and is characterized by high productivity rates and state investment, which led to the establishing of modern welfare provisions.

At its core, the postwar era peculiarly consisted in the affirmation of a societal model based on work as the bedrock of social cohesion. Stable, permanent employment represented the structure of certainty for many in their aspirations and life plans. The affluency granted by jobs, in turn, was instrumental to foster mass consumption practices. Following the transition from Taylorism to Fordism between the late 1800s and the early 1900s, industrial capitalism in the postwar era was finally able to cater for the standardized production of large quantities of commodities, sold on the market of an emergent "consumer society." Jobs, mainly in cities or nearby suburbs, available to many, usually for life, led the same many to afford purchasing the goods produced by the industry. The concomitant rise of mass media provided the tools to display these commodities and perpetuate a steady demand. Propelled by advertising, that taught consumers what to buy and how, this societal model developed into an ideal for a living. The myth of upwards social mobility incarnated by the American Dream translated into a set of prescriptive practices to live the "good life" of working and consuming. Stereotypically described, this consists in the smooth succession of: finding a job, getting married, purchasing a house (and stocking it with consumer appliances), having kids and then retiring approximately at the same time one's kids will have had kids. As a societal model, it grew strong because...well, it worked. For a while, at least. Quite importantly, it was simple and easy to relate to. It offered comfort, structure and confidence in the future of generations to come. Yet, this translated into the somewhat generalized expectation that the social conditions experienced during that time were immutable and inevitably destined to be *everyone's* social condition ever after. However, things were about to change, and in a much different direction.

In 1971, the US unilaterally broke the Bretton Woods agreement, which tied the price of gold to the value of the dollar. A global recession followed, bringing the Golden Age of Capitalism to an abrupt close. This marks a typical trait in Arrighi's accumulation cycles model: the mid-cycle crisis, a milestone that signals the transition to a phase of financial expansion. Furthermore, it coincided with the affirmation of a set of policies that came to be known as the economic, social, cultural and political project of *neoliberalism*. This affirmed as hegemonic across the Western world in the late 1970s and then into the 1980s and 1990s, being widely experimented with in the US, the UK and elsewhere, often presented as *the only alternative*. The neoliberal doctrine dictated to prioritize economic profit upon anything else, promoting entrepreneurial success as an ideological proposition and envisaging a society "made of individuals," as the British PM and neoliberal champion Margaret Thatcher famously proclaimed. The affirmation of neoliberalism pivoted a phase of hard-core globalization, which resulted in the proliferation of transnational, finance-driven economic institutions, large-scale deregulation policies and a generalized distrust for the nation-state.[5] Yet the most significant changes brought along by the neoliberal era concern the way we conceive of, practice and think about *work*.

In parallel with the emphasis on entrepreneurship and individual economic action, neoliberal policies consistently eroded the stability of employment. Work in the neoliberal age became "flexible," increasingly precarious and atypical, exuding from its usual spaces and blurring the boundaries between leisure and productive time. Practices of outsourcing were accompanied by a large-scale devaluation of labor (i.e., lowering salaries), considered as the main pathway to profitability for companies in a competitive global economy. Then, toward the late 1990s and early 2000s, this blended with the affirmation of the Internet, which allowed new modes of working to emerge, and others to transform or disappear. The skyrocketing costs of education, coupled with the limited availability of job opportunities and their ordinary precarity, caused many to reshape their career and life expectations, often forcing processes of migration from one country to another and inducing many to tune their lifestyles in accordance with the new economy.

Then, the 2007-8 economic crash happened. The shrinking of financial markets worldwide, combined with the long-term consequences of globalization, brought a spike in unemployment figures across the Western world. Finding a job became all the more difficult, and when one had a job, in many cases it was unfulfilling or insufficient to make a living. While work is admittedly everywhere – go to any Starbucks, one might say, and you'll easily find many people who work in front of their laptops – employment isn't. The American journalist and writer Sarah Kendzior labels this scenario as an emergent "post-employment economy." The simple act of working, she writes, no longer means having a job. The mere fact of having a job no longer means making a living, while the number of "working poors" – people who work but do not make enough money for a living – incessantly grows.[6]

This has created a widespread sense of resentment, particularly (but not solely) among older generations, for a society that defies established expectations of social mobility. This reflects into a generalized distrust for the liberal order that had promised to give everyone a chance at living the "good life," making room for disengagement, anger and fear. As work ceases to be the bedrock around which one's adult life can be built, a condition that was long considered acquired and immutable, enter nostalgia: in their longing for a time that can't return, the Brexit and Trump votes ratify the end of the "long" twentieth century.

"Unelected nostalgia breeds monsters"

Usually nostalgia is rather innocuous. We think back to our teenage and our first love experiences, the music we listened to and the movies we loved. We reminisce about the time we stayed out until late or watched the dawn rise from atop a hill, while our parents thought we'd be home soon. We long for the day we left home and never actually made it to school, and the sense of freedom it bore. Sometimes we are nostalgic about things or events we *haven't* actually lived – Arjun Appadurai calls it "imagined nostalgia."[7] But a remarkable aspect of nostalgia is that it is at once a deeply individual and a shared sentiment. We regularly bring up memories in conversations with friends. We do so for those to be actually meaningful, for us and our interlocutors, but also because that's one of the most effective ways (sometimes the only way) we can actually relate to one another – not by means of what we are living, but of what we have lived. Although we can be nostalgic alone, for the most part we aren't. Nostalgia is, at its core, a way of togetherness.[8]

Yet, the imaginary travel in memory that characterizes nostalgia is a journey that takes one backwards but also forwards. It often transforms the past into the illusion of a future. By mythologizing the past, nostalgia provides with a sometimes unconscious, sometimes conscious vision of the past as a place to return to. Nostalgia entails the reassuring pleasure of dreaming about an impossible return to when things were simpler and happier. It brings back to a non-existent land that suddenly appears again within reach, not physically but emotionally, offering comfort and healing. At its core, nostalgia is a populist sentiment, an emotional shortcut that appeals to the heart, rather than the mind.

Because of its fascinating traits, nostalgia has long been a topic of significant interest for intellectuals of various kinds. Literary theorist Svetlana Boym recounts how the word "nostalgia" first appears in writing as part of the medical dissertation of a Swiss doctor, Thomas Hofer, in 1688. Back then, it was considered the "disease of an afflicted imagination," diagnosed to soldiers, exiles and migrants who were separated from their families and longed for the home soil. Accordingly, nostalgia was cured as an illness by psychologists and psychiatrists, who prescribed herbs, "warm hypnotic emulsions" and sometimes opium as a remedy to homesickness.[9]

Later, however, nostalgia got deeply entrenched with modernity. Fredric Jameson names it as a key feature of the postmodern era, in its manifestations across various forms of cultural production.[10] Historian Gary Cross underlines the inextricable relationship between nostalgia and consumer culture, as nostalgia makes us crave for the objects and the music of our youth.[11] At the start of the twenty-first century, I argue, nostalgia has germinated into a large-scale societal *zeitgeist*, the most visible symptom of the current pathologies of capitalism. "The 20th century began with a futuristic utopia and ended with nostalgia," notes Boym. "The optimistic belief in the future has become outmoded," she continues, "while nostalgia, for better or for worse, never went out of fashion, remaining uncannily contemporary."[12]

Also *The Economist* proclaims: we are experiencing a global outbreak of nostalgia.[13] Trump and Brexit, of course: but also China, that aspires return to its own golden age; Mexico and Italy, where populist politicians from the left (Mexico) and the right (Italy) won groundbreaking elections calling for a restoration of "national sovereignty"; Brazil, where the rise of

Jair Bolsonaro brought the far right to the presidency; Hungary and Poland, where right-wing governments work toward the restoration of traditional values; Germany, where AfD – Alternative fur Deutschland – poses a threat to the Christian Democrat centrist hegemony. Albeit with different nuances, the appearance of these populist parties represents a reaction across the board to the decline of the Western societal model of the postwar era, wrapped in a claim against globalism and the economic and cultural elites. The most disconcerting aspect in this nostalgic outbreak is its frightening correspondence with the surge of old and new right-wing movements, which took the occasion to reclaim long-lost relevance. The revival of typical nationalist tropes, such as anti-foreigner sentiment – foreigners steal our jobs! – or antisemitism, is also a strong element of this populist, nostalgic era.

The dangerous nature of this "regressive nostalgia" is well described by Zygmunt Bauman in his last book, *Retrotopia*. Bauman grasps with characteristic, unique clarity the loss of the shared sense of community and of the idea of progress that characterized the rise of modernity – which, Bauman argues, has been "privatized" by neoliberalism. This, Bauman concludes, ignites a "retro-topian" dream to return to the communitarian spirit incarnated by nation-states. This surprises us because, despite it has some historical precedents, yet for some reason we thought it would never happen again.[14] Bauman's argument draws heavily from Boym, who argues that nostalgia offers a kind of "longing" that is often misunderstood for "belonging" – and henceforth quickly turns into a drive towards national communities and "pure homelands." Boym writes:

> Álgia (longing) is what we share, yet nóstos (the return home) is what divides us. It is the promise to rebuild the ideal home that lies at the core of many powerful ideologies of today, tempting us to relinquish critical thinking for emotional

bonding. The danger of nostalgia is that it tends to confuse the actual home with an imaginary one. In extreme cases, it can create a phantom homeland, for the sake of which one is ready to die or kill. Unelected nostalgia breeds monsters. Yet the sentiment itself, the mourning of displacement and temporal irreversibility, is at the very core of the modern condition.[15]

A remarkable trait of twenty-first century nostalgia is its vivid presence in everyday popular culture. Music critic Simon Reynolds called it a "retromania":[16] from the return into fashion of vinyl records, that almost everybody considered outdated in the early 1990s and are instead made again objects of a cult of possession, to the remakes of decades-old TV shows such as *Twin Peaks* or *Gilmore Girls*, and the periodic reformation of music acts from previous decades, pop culture today is paramount nostalgic. (As I write these lines, *Bohemian Rhapsody*, the movie about Queen singer Freddie Mercury, is reported to have won four Academy Awards). However, this "retromania" is more than just a safe bet for the culture industry to invest in products and protagonists of the popular culture of the past that still sell well. In fact, it is a conspicuous feature also of the popular culture born in this day and age. Think about TV series such as *Stranger Things,* which is a trove of memorabilia, songs and references from the 1980s, or *13 Reasons Why,* a teenage drama based on the recovery of a box of audio cassettes recorded by a teenage girl who committed suicide, yet set in the age of smartphones and social media. Take a walk into teenage fast fashion stores such as Brandy Melville or Primark, and you will find t-shirts with prints of music stars from the 1990s, such as Nirvana or Metallica, proudly worn by young teenagers born in the early 2000s who likely have no clue about who Nirvana or Metallica actually are. Nostalgia is such a key component in promotional practices today that a specific term – *retromarketing* – has come into use. We are drowning in nostalgia. It is all around us and in everyone's most mundane conversations.

But there's more. "Outbreaks of nostalgia often follow revolutions," notes Svetlana Boym.[17] This was the case for the French revolution in 1789, as well as the Russian revolution of 1917 – and in some sense it is also today. We are in fact in the middle of a revolution: thanks to digital technologies, social media and smartphones, we are witnessing a radical rupture in the ways in which we work, consume, socialize, go on a date, form our political opinion, access the news, debate, vote, book a holiday – a transformation that was somewhat sudden, and which large parts of the population find hard to understand or make sense of. Think about it: almost none of these technologies existed before 2007. Facebook existed, but was just about to become a global sensation. The iPhone, Airbnb, Uber – all come in, or soon after, 2007. Incidentally (or not?), the same year of the economic crash.[18] Nostalgia, in other words, is a cultural marker of societal turning points.

Social media, in particular, significantly contributed to the rise of the current nostalgic zeitgeist. Countless Facebook pages drive millions of people every day to share memories of their adolescence and collectively reminisce about something. Instagram, with its retro-aesthetics, makes every picture look as if it was taken in the 1980s (I often wonder what Roland Barthes would say about Instagram!). YouTube hosts an almost infinite repertoire of videos from the past, that are regularly commented by users who create imagined communities around the music or the TV shows of their youth. All this is paradoxical, Reynolds suggests: as we are immersed in advanced information technologies, from smartphones to social media, we largely use these as time machines.[19]

Nonetheless, social media has become the main terrain upon which today's hegemonic nostalgic sentiment has bred and continues to prosper. While digital technologies have offered unprecedented possibilities of socializing and networking, they have also come to represent dangerous instruments of public opinion manipulation, power and propaganda. Their functioning favors polarization of opinion, personalization of information, the creation of "filter bubbles," the spread of fake news and the systematic diminishing of expertise, now that all knowledge is believed to be at a Google search distance. This amplifies the sense of estrangement from the present that affects parts of the Western society, so that the innocuous nostalgia we usually experience when we get old has turned into a more complex societal dispute. "When there was paper..." regularly laments my father, a somewhat stereotypical Baby Boomer, when he talks about the Internet. It is no coincidence that Baby Boomers are reported to be the most relevant demographic in the Brexit and Trump votes, and are significantly more likely to share fake news irrespective of their political affiliation.[20] But it's not just Baby Boomers: a new kind of culture war, that heavily involves also the youngest generations, seems to be taking place in the "new social" of the Internet around some of the socially progressive achievements of the twentieth century, such as multiculturalism, sexual diversity and the right to abortion. The distrust in science, the rise of conspiracy theories, the crusade against political correctness and gender equality, the rise of subcultural spaces that project masculinity as the epitome of strength and want to relegate women to an inferior role in society – like the *incel* ("involuntary celibate") communities – are all phenomena underpinned by a more or less explicit, populist nostalgic dimension, that finds a new home – and a megaphone – in the weirdest corners of the online world.[21]

* * *

But this "regressive nostalgia" is only one side of the story.

* * *

At the same time that the discontent about work and the global economy fuels the conservative reactions of Brexit and Trump, other segments of society experiment with alternatives. While many continue to aspire to the ideal of the "good life" of the twentieth century, in the debris of neoliberalism we can witness the contours of a potentially different societal model in the making, constituted of practices of working and consuming that set as explicitly alternative to the environmentally unsustainable industrial capitalist model of the postwar times. Yet, some of these equally look back for inspiration – *further back*, to revive craft production techniques from a pre-industrial era and turn them into small-scale, "fair" consumption endeavors, particularly in the food industry, that stand in radical opposition to industrialization.[22] Epitomized by the affirmation of hipster culture, this kind of "progressive nostalgia" is also a key feature of the start of the twenty-first century. As an ambivalent and nuanced concept, nostalgia allows to reconcile these opposite phenomena within the same framework. I will argue that, despite its inherent contradictions, hipster culture represents an attempt at developing a new ideal of the "good life" in the post-employment era, that seeks to move beyond the interlocking relationship between jobs for life and mass consumption which represented the social pact upon which twentieth century prosperity was built. We'll see all this, and more, in the pages that follow.

Two disclaimers

First. I am a sociologist, but this is only in part a sociological book – not just in style, but also in substance. If this was a full-fledged sociological work, it would be more empirically-driven and grounded in first-hand data. It would unpack theories, develop hypotheses, struggle with concepts and methods more than it actually does. This book, on the contrary, is a semi-sociological, pop observation of the times we are living; therefore, it should be taken as an unstructured walk into twenty-first century nostalgia. It is based upon experiences, travels, discussions and snippets of real life as much as it relies on social theory and empirical data. It draws from popular culture as much as it does from scholarly work, as it wants to be of interest for academics and everyday readers alike. Ultimately, it is unapologetically a very Western book, because it seeks to describe the current pathologies of capitalism from the perspective I inhabit and know best.

Second. This book does not want to be judgmental on nostalgia as a sentiment. I am not against nostalgia per se, although I am not a nostalgic by personality. Like many, I am not immune to forms of consumer nostalgia: I regularly buy books from second-hand bookshops, and most of the music I listen to belongs to the past, particularly the 1980s and 1990s (but I am not an extremist: there is good music today too). I consider the 1990s the happiest time there has ever been to be alive, but I'm aware that that's the time of my teenage, so this is a very biased perception – in fact, the 1990s were not necessarily better per se in any particular way than other decades. I don't believe there is anywhere we should all aim to return to, but I appreciate some people do, and I am interested in learning more about what brings them to longing for the past, and why. I don't write about society being in decay only because I get older, and I don't think some kind of digital technology will come and save us (no, not even blockchain). If you're ok with these premises, then read on.

Notes

[1]   Mark Fisher, *Capitalist realism: is there no alternative?* Zero Books: John Hunt Publishing, 2009, pp. 1-12.

[2]   Edgar Morin, *L'esprit du temps.* Paris, Grasset, 1962.

[3]   Giovanni Arrighi, *The long twentieth century: Money, power,*

and the origins of our times. London: Verso, 1994.

[4] Stephen A. Marglin and Juliet B. Schor (Eds.), *The golden age of capitalism: reinterpreting the postwar experience.* New York: Oxford University Press, 1990.

[5] On neoliberalism, see David Harvey, *A brief history of neoliberalism.* New York: Oxford University Press, 2007.

[6] Sarah Kendzior, *The view from flyover country: dispatches from the forgotten America.* New York: Flatiron Books, 2018.

[7] Arjun Appadurai, *Modernity at large: cultural dimensions of globalization* (Vol. 1). Minneapolis: University of Minnesota Press, 1996.

[8] There is ample literature on nostalgia, from different scholarly perspectives. On the relationship between nostalgia and identity, see: Fred Davis, *Yearning for yesterday: a sociology of nostalgia.* Florence, MA: Free Press, 1996; Janelle L. Wilson, *Nostalgia: sanctuary of Meaning.* Lewisburg, PA: Bucknell University Press, 2005.

[9] Svetlana Boym, *The future of nostalgia.* New York: Basic Books, 2008, pp. 19-20.

[10] Fredric Jameson, *Postmodernism, or, the cultural logic of late capitalism.* Durham, NC: Duke University Press, 1991.

[11] Gary Cross, *Consumed nostalgia: memory in the age of fast capitalism.* New York: Columbia University Press, 2015.

[12] Svetlana Boym, *Nostalgia,* 2011. Available at: http://monumenttotransformation.org/atlas-of-transformation/html/n/nostalgia/nostalgia-svetlana-boym.html (Last accessed 24 July 2019).

[13] 'The world is fixated on the past," *The Economist,* 2018. Available at: https://www.economist.com/leaders/2018/12/22/the-world-is-fixated-on-the-past (Last accessed 12 April 2019).

[14] Zygmunt Bauman, *Retrotopia.* London: Polity, 2017, p. 5.

[15] Svetlana Boym, *The future of nostalgia.* New York: Basic Books, 2008, p. 12.

[16] Simon Reynolds, *Retromania: pop culture's addiction to its own past*. London: Faber and Faber, 2011.

[17] See Svetlana Boym, *The future of nostalgia*. New York: Basic Books, 2008, p. 12; Zygmunt Bauman, *Retrotopia*. London: Polity, 2017, p. 10.

[18] Thomas L. Friedman, *Thank you for being late: an optimist's guide to thriving in the age of accelerations*. New York: Picador, 2017.

[19] Simon Reynolds, *Retromania: Pop culture's addiction to its own past*. London: Faber and Faber, 2011.

[20] Andrew Guess, Jonathan Nagler and Joshua Tucker, "Less than you think: prevalence and predictors of fake news dissemination on Facebook." *Science advances*, 5(1), 2019. Available at: https://advances.sciencemag.org/content/5/1/eaau4586 (Last accessed 1 July 2019).

[21] See: Angela Nagle, *Kill all normies: online culture wars from 4chan and Tumblr to Trump and the alt-right*. Zero Books: John Hunt Publishing, 2017; Elle Reeve, "This is what the life of an incel looks like," *Vice magazine*, 2017. Available at: https://news.vice.com/en_us/article/7xqw3g/this-is-what-the-life-of-an-incel-looks-like?utm_source=vicefbus (Last accessed 22 July 2019).

[22] Richard E. Ocejo, *Masters of craft: old jobs in the new urban economy*. Princeton, NY: Princeton University Press, 2017.

2. The "good life"

All over people changing their votes
Along with their overcoats
If Adolf Hitler flew in today
They'd send a limousine anyway
The Clash, White Man in Hammersmith Palais

Take Back Control, recites the famous Brexit slogan. Control on what? Back to where?

* * *

London is a bubble of 8 million people, with 37 percent of its residents born outside of the UK and more than 300 different languages spoken every day. All but five London boroughs voted to remain in the European Union in the 2016 referendum. The biggest chunk of Leave votes in London came from Havering, the farthest of the eastern boroughs, home of the towns of Romford and Upminster. Based on the 2011 UK census, we know that Havering has a largely white demographic (88 percent); together with Bromley, it is the least diverse borough in the Greater London area. Bexley, second among London boroughs per number of Leave votes, borders Havering on the south side and largely shares the same demographic composition. The borough of Barking and Dagenham, third in London per number of Leave votes, borders Havering on the western side.

Between 2001 and 2011, the resident population of Havering grew a good 14 percent less than the average London borough, and its average age is 5 percent older. Havering hosts a significantly higher number of people in the age range 65-84 and 84+ compared to London and the rest of the UK. Havering is mostly composed of pensioners and married couples and has the lowest percentage of same-sex civil partnerships in London (less than half). In 2011, a sizable 16 percent of working-age Havering residents had no educational qualifications; the average weekly earnings for a Havering resident were £566.60, a figure that is higher than most parts of England but lower than the London average. The Socio-Economic Profile Report published in January 2013 concludes that "(i)n addition to the changing demographic, diversity and socio-economic profile of Havering's population, the economic downturn has both exacerbated existing issues the borough faces and introduced new challenges such as local government and third sector funding cuts."[1] Put differently, Havering is a metaphor of the Brexit vote: the more you go out of London, the more you will find an economically-strained, less-ethnically diverse and increasingly aging population, scared of what the global economy has brought to their courtyards. The Leave vote is, in other words, a kick back at this social and economic anxiety.

In the public perception, Brexit is first and foremost about one key issue: immigration. For many Brexiters, exiting the European Union primarily means putting a halt to the freedom of movement of people coming into the UK from European countries, especially from the Eastern European bloc and the Mediterranean, considered as job stealers and "health tourists" who take advantage of the UK system of benefits and of the National Health System, free at the point of access. Yet, interestingly many of the areas where the Leave vote was larger are also areas that do *not* experience immigration and multiculturalism that much. Records seem to show a clear trend: the lower the number of non-British, non-white residents in a certain area, the higher the pro-Brexit percentage. It is the fear of immigration, more than immigration itself, that drove many to vote for Brexit.[2]

Arguably, the twenty-first century has brought about a renewed fear of the stranger. This has longstanding roots, but to a large extent is a long-term consequence of the discourse on Islam that animated the West after 9/11. In *Retrotopia*, Zygmunt Bauman argued that we are witnessing the resurrection of a tribal mentality for which, "(a) neighborhood filled by strangers is a visible, tangible sign of certainties evaporating (...) Strangers stand for everything evasive, feeble, unstable and unforeseeable in life."[3] The fear of the stranger is a key component of the nostalgia that breeds monsters. In the months after the referendum, the UK Metropolitan Police recorded a 49 percent increase in hate crime across England, Wales and Northern Ireland.[4] I, for one, also was a victim of hate crime, on the Saturday night after the vote, when a mentally-ill person overheard us talk in Italian on the bus that was taking us home, and enthusiastically told us that, yes, actually, finally we were about to, "go back to your fucking country."

The anger and tribal divisions that characterize the nostalgic fantasy of Brexit sowed violence not just against strangers, but against whoever does not think alike. The vile murder of pro-European Labour MP Jo Cox, killed by a white supremacist with a history of mental health issues named Thomas Alexander Mair in the run-up to the 2016 EU referendum, shows this at its most dangerous. Mair brutally killed Cox outside of a local library in West Yorkshire because he considered her a representative of the liberal, "globalist" left, which together with mainstream media he considered the "cause of all evil." In his eyes, Cox as a supporter of European Union membership, was an advocate of unregulated immigration and henceforth a "traitor" to the United Kingdom as a country. The rhetoric of Brexit as a patriotic act unleashed the monster of racism in the UK, legitimizing its rise. It is imbued of this rhetoric that, on 19 June 2017, a man named Darren Osborne hired a van in Cardiff and drove it all the way to Finsbury Park in London, on the same day, to run over a crowd of worshippers exiting the local mosque at midnight after the prayer – killing one and injuring many others.[5]

Yet a sole focus on immigration actually hides the other tightly-related and equally relevant issues that contributed to the appeal of Brexit as a nostalgic calling. In fact, Brexit is about immigration as much as it is about the consequences of globalization and more than a decade of austerity economics. It is about the difficulty by the generations that lived most of their adult life in the second half of the twentieth century to understand how the world has changed, and the perception that what they achieved over that period is now being lost forever. To fully understand Brexit, jobs and the economy but also education and age matter just as much as immigration does. "Brexit is the consequence of the economic bargain struck in the early 1980s," writes *Guardian* journalist John Harris the day after the referendum, "whereby we waved goodbye to the security and certainties of the postwar settlement, and were given instead an economic model that has just about served the most populous parts of the country, while leaving too much of the rest to anxiously decline." "What defines these furies," Harris continues:

> is often clear enough: a terrible shortage of homes, an impossibly precarious job market, a too-often overlooked sense that men (and men are particularly relevant here) who would once have been certain in their identity as miners, or steelworkers, now feel demeaned and ignored. The attempts of mainstream politics to still the anger have probably only made it worse: oily tributes to "hardworking families," or the fingers-down-a-blackboard trope of "social mobility," with its suggestion that the only thing Westminster can offer working-class people is a specious chance of not being working class anymore.

* * *

Brexit is more than the EU, Harris concludes. It is about inequality and class war simmering below the surface for decades, that ultimately found a voice in the nostalgic utopia of a nationalist outbreak. As an interviewee in the same article synthesizes: "If you've got money, you vote in. If you haven't got money, you vote out."[6]

* * *

Travel to the other side of the pond, America, and you'll find a similar story. *Make America Great Again*, shouts the typical Trump's red hat voter. "Again" as in what, exactly? The 2016 Trump campaign is a glamourous example of nationalist and ugly anti-migrant rhetoric, exemplified by the regular "build the wall" chants that dominated Trump's rallies. Similar to Brexit, the Trump rise unleashed a return of white nationalism – now rebranded as the "alt-right" – that emerged as a newly legitimized right-wing discourse in the national debate. For one, take the infamous Charlottesville protests in August 2017, which saw 21-year-old neo-Nazi James Field kill peaceful protester Heather Meyer. How did Trump react? He commented on the events describing parts of the neo-Nazi crowd as "very fine people," and accounting for "blame on both sides."[7] To the joy of neo-Nazis, of course.

But Trump's success and continuing support from his base can only in part be explained by his affiliation to the ultra-nationalist, white supremacist right. His appeal runs deeper in American society by means of a potent railing against the disappearing of jobs and the decay of how "great" America used to be in the twentieth century. The calling to a pre-global society based on stable employment is at the heart of Trump's "make America Great Again" slogan. America is "great again," in the Trump discourse, if it comes back to being the predominantly white, patriarchal industrial society that it was in the postwar times. Railing against the "globalist" liberal elite who want "open borders," Trump also advocates for neo-isolationist policies to halt globalization as a process that takes jobs away from the US homeland. During his 2016 campaign, he traveled regularly to former industrial towns of the Midwest, where deindustrialization hit the hardest on local communities who relied on industrial jobs to pay their rent, promising to create new "old" jobs for coal workers and miners. Take this excerpt from a speech Trump delivered, incidentally just a few days after the Brexit vote, from a metal recycling facility in Pennsylvania, the heart of the Rust Belt, an area where many factories have closed down over the last decades:

> We are thirty miles from Steel City. Pittsburgh played a central role in building our nation. The legacy of Pennsylvania steelworkers lives in the bridges, railways and skyscrapers that make up our great American landscape. But our workers' loyalty was repaid with betrayal. Our politicians have aggressively pursued a policy of globalization – moving our jobs, our wealth and our factories to Mexico and overseas. Globalization has made the financial elite who donate to politicians very wealthy. But it has left millions of our workers with nothing but poverty and heartache. When subsidized foreign steel is dumped into our markets, threatening our factories, the politicians do nothing. For years, they watched on the sidelines as our jobs vanished and our communities were plunged into depression-level unemployment. Many of these areas have still never recovered. Our politicians took away from the people their means of making a living and supporting their families. Skilled craftsmen and tradespeople and factory workers have seen the jobs they loved shipped thousands of miles away. Many Pennsylvania towns once thriving and humming are now in a state of despair. This wave of globalization has wiped out our *middle class*.[8]

This message resounded conspicuously in particular among working-class workers in states such as Michigan, Pennsylvania and Wisconsin, whose votes tipped the Electoral College in Trump's direction and awarded him the presidency. There, despite Barack Obama's rescue of Chrysler in 2010, Democrats are largely seen as the party of the professional elite, made of rich and posh city swaggers who live lives that are perceived to be galaxies away from the constraints of working-class folks. Despite his millionaire status, in the 2016 election Trump was able to successfully project himself as a champion for the rural and deindustrialized populations of the Midwest, enough at least to secure his election. His appeal is also partly owed to his celebrity status and the aspirational dimension the figure of the millionaire still carries for the American working-class, as well as to being a white man with a builder identity – just like for Brexit, in Trump's message men are indeed particularly relevant. Law professor Joan Williams underlines how the US working class mythologizes the rich, while resenting the poor and the professional class alike. Their dream is not to join the upper middle class, but to stay true to the traditional values of their own communities.[9] Blend this with their marked distrust for Hillary Clinton, a woman (yet again, a woman) who perfectly represented the professional liberal elite of Washington politics, and there you have it. In short: Trump and Brexit should be seen as the megaphones of the anger against the demise of the ideal of the "good life" of work and consumption that characterizes the societal model of the twentieth century.

The "good life": the middle class ideal for a living

The twentieth century postwar era is marked up by the affirmation of the "white-collar" middle class. This is a social category composed by individuals employed as salaried workers, usually in office occupations, who have college education and can enjoy a level of affluency that is superior to that of those employed in manual and menial work, but not up to the one the upper classes can afford. In the second half of the twentieth century, the white-collar middle class came to embody the myth of upwards social mobility of the American Dream. A pseudo-ideological narration based on meritocracy and work, the American Dream branded America to the rest of the Western world as the place in which every individual, irrespective of one's origins, is afforded the possibility to "work their way up" through the social ladder. As synthesized by Barack Obama in a 2013 speech, this is "middle-class America's basic bargain, that if you work hard, you have a chance to get ahead."[10]

As a result of their affluency, the emergent middle class of the 1950s and 1960s enthusiastically embraced the then-emergent consumer economy, which soon became an aspirational battleground for social status for the whole of society. One's class status in the postwar era was perceived to be a reflection of one's occupation and the possibility to afford certain consumer goods – most commonly a house, a car and technologically-advanced home appliances. At the same time, work in the postwar era became the key marker of one's identity. Owed to this prospering economic period, this societal model quickly affirmed into an ideal for a living, based on stable employment as a structure of certainty and the conduit to living a "good life."

In general terms, the concept of the "good life" dates back to Greek philosophy, when it meant living a life of leisure and virtue, a life of health, prosperity and good luck, a life of social recognition for one's achievements. Sociologist Hartmut Rosa underlines how there is no binding consensus in modern societies as to what living a "good life" means. Its definition, Rosa underlines, has become "the most intimately private matter of all things." Yet, he contends, there is societal agreement as to the *precondition* for living a good life, which is to "secure the resources you might need for living your dream (whatever that might be!)." This, Rosa suggests, has become "the overruling rational imperative of modernity," an "aspiration to acquire the resources necessary or helpful for" living a good life. The significance of this imperative is all the more testified by the proliferation of self-help books in recent years, that promise to be practical guides to *anything*: happiness, health, wealth, romance and much more.[11] The precondition to a "good life" in the second half of the twentieth century, in simple terms, is having a job.

In the definition given by Lauren Berlant in *Cruel Optimism*, the "good life" ideal of the twentieth century consists in the capacity to live a "capitalist life."[12] The "good life" in the postwar era is a life of working and consuming, that entails both a symbolic and practical dimension. On the one hand, it is a life that revolves around the possession of permanent, stable, full-time employment. Epitomized by the 9-to-5 routine, the "good life" of the twentieth century is first and foremost a life *made of,* and *constructed around,* work – a life whose rhythms and spaces overlap with those of work, and where a clear separation between productive time and leisure time is drawn. In this sense it is a life constructed around the man's work, as men are most often the breadwinners, while women engage in domestic labor, taking care of the family and the house. At the same time, the twentieth century "good life" demands an enthusiastic subscription to the consumer economy, for that work provides with the means to engage in the purchase, possession and display of goods which, in turn, generate social status and recognition. In the "good life" ideal, being a good worker and a good consumer are, ultimately, two sides of the same coin. A good worker is one who staunchly labors to produce – one who does not complain, for that the not complaining will be rewarded, with a salary, or a promotion, or a raise. Yet a good worker must also be a good consumer – one who does not refrain from consuming, for that the option of not consuming is somewhat against the capitalist vision of progress that the "good life" ideal puts into practice.

Consumption historian Lizabeth Cohen notes that the US

necessitated to foster an enthusiastic embrace of the consumer economy in the aftermath of World War II to the aim of ensuring the US would continue to prosper beyond a phase of large military spending. Thus, consumption was framed as a "civic responsibility" to the whole of American society: "What you buy and how you buy it is very vital in your new life – and to our whole American way of living." Cohen describes this as the creation of a "consumers republic," whereby consumption practices were packaged with an allure of equality and social mobility, for all Americans to aspire to own mass-produced goods irrespective of their social origins. A peculiar role in the consumers republic, Cohen argues, is held by home ownership: "One out of every four homes standing in the United States in 1960 went up in the 1950s. As a result of this explosion in house construction, by the same year, 62 percent of Americans could claim that they owned their own homes, in contrast to only 44 percent as recently as 1940 (the biggest jump in home ownership rates ever recorded)." This was made possible also thanks to the assistance of the central government, in the form of low mortgage interests and tax cuts, designed to ensure the broadest possible participation in the emergent new world of consumption.[13]

Incarnated by America, a powerful imaginary and prescriptive ideal for upwards social mobility affirmed across Western society in the postwar era. This was rooted in the *belief* in modernity and progress and based on the entangling of work and consumption as a social pact for the future. Its hegemonic symbolic regime, I argue, is an overlooked aspect in today's analyses of the nostalgic outbreak. There is, in fact, a generation who grew up in the middle of this imaginary, who went into the world with the task of putting it into practice and believed the societal model they experienced was *the only* possible one. Then, when the time came to pass it on to their kids and grandkids, they began to experience its demise. These are the Baby Boomers.

Educated to the "good life": the Baby Boomers

"Born at the right time": this is how Canadian historian Doug Owram[14] describes the generation known as the Baby Boomers. Usually categorized as those born between the mid-1940s and the late 1960s, Baby Boomers have been hailed as the protagonists of the second half of the twentieth century, being synonymous with the Golden Age of Capitalism. Their iconic name finds reason in the spike of births that took place in the West following World War II: the US census, for one, accounts that around 79 million Americans belong to the Baby Boomers generation. Similarly high figures in birth rates were recorded also in other parts of the Western world.[15]

Despite this categorization, here I do not seek to establish firm boundaries between one generation and another. In fact, the sociology of generation is a contested terrain: many have stressed how generation theories do not adequately explain key social variables in terms of, for instance, class inequality or job satisfaction.[16] Yet, I contend there is truth in the argument that cohorts of people who grew up roughly at the same time actually share an imaginary and a set of experiences that mark, from a cultural perspective, their perceived belonging to a certain group. In this sense, I use here Monika Krause's notion of "zeitgeist" as a tool for sociological analysis. Krause argues that a zeitgeist can be observed as a "pattern in meaningful practices that is specific to a particular historical time-period, links different realms of social life and social groups, and extends across geographical contexts." Hence, Krause continues, "the concept of zeitgeist sensitises us to a set of phenomena, which can be described independently of and alongside other cultural phenomena such as trans-historical schemas, binaries or group-specific patterns."[17] The generational labels – Baby Boomers and, later, Generation X and Millennials – that appear in this book, in other words, should actually be seen as conventions that identify specific cultural zeitgeists, related to the time-period when certain commonly-conceived cohorts have grown up immersed in a shared set of meanings, symbols and objects, which have arguably shaped their sense of identity and their relationship with the outside world. Accordingly, it may be argued that Western Baby Boomers grew up in the middle of a very peculiar zeitgeist. Janelle Wilson notes that:

> the Baby Boomers, as a generation that had a number of defining events (such as the Vietnam War; the assassinations of John F. Kennedy, Robert Kennedy, Jr., and Martin Luther King, Jr.; the Women's Movement; the Civil Rights Movement), can be said to have a distinct generational identity. Members of this generation have many cultural resources to draw from in maintaining a sense of collective identity. Boomers came of age during a time of major social, political and world events. Given their impressionable age, members of this generation surely were affected by these events.[18]

Yet, despite the Cold War and the social conflicts around, for instance, racial segregation and gender inequality that marked their juvenile years, Baby Boomers as a cohort had the luck to become adults in times of optimism, opportunity and abundance. Usually portrayed as a traditional nuclear family, clearly divided by gender roles (he works, she cooks), engaged in community service and/or religious practices,[19] Baby Boomers are those who benefited the most from the favorable economic conjuncture of the postwar years. Growing up in an era of optimism, Baby Boomers experienced what was perceived as a democratization of social mobility. A good number of them enjoyed a relative ease of access to stable jobs and income: the US Bureau of Labor Statistics reports that the number of white-collar workers increased by 9 million between 1960 and 1970, with an increase in total employment figures between 65.8 million to 78.6 million workers (a 20 percent increase in a decade).[20]

Over the same period, Baby Boomers were educated to the capitalist "good life" of work and consumption. The affirmation of the set of principles and values at the heart of the "good life" ideal of the postwar era was facilitated by the emergent relevance of mass media; in particular, advertising is argued to have held a key role in this educational endeavor. One of the key theorists of the postindustrial society, Daniel Bell, argued in 1957 that advertising presented a set of "detailed instructions on how to live," which aimed "to teach people how to dress, to furnish a home, the wines to put away, the cheeses to cultivate – in short, the style of life appropriate to the new middle class status."[21] Advertising has been seen as responsible for a shift in values in the postwar era, as it promoted aspirational consumption as a practice of primary importance and contributed to spread a cult of the material good.[22] While we should not see its effects in a deterministic fashion, arguably advertising significantly contributed to the creation of the imaginary that underpins the "good life" ideal, and to its long-lasting success. Consumer scholars Russell Belk and Richard Pollay suggest to see advertising "as a significant factor in reinforcing and strengthening the life it portrays." In a research that looked at the history of magazine advertising by decade, between 1900 and 1980, they found that advertising in the postwar era "increasingly employed pleasure, luxury and terminal materialism to sell their products and services."[23]

To take a view at the symbolic imaginary the Baby Boomers grew up in, take the famous *Icons* book on American ads in the 1960s, which hosts a trove of print ads from that era. These illustrate well the prescribed features of the "good life" ideal. Men – almost exclusively white – are usually portrayed in professional suits, to emphasize their role as breadwinners; when in the house, they are immersed in scenes of after-work leisure, often surrounded by modern consumer appliances. Women, on the other hand, are commonly depicted either in some activity considered as typically "feminine," such as hair drying, or working in the domestic environment – mainly in the kitchen. Oftentimes, women are all but a decorative element in the scene, serving to promote fashion goods or purely to attract the male gaze; other times they are a supporting character, tasked with aiding or staring at "the man" while he does some kind of dangerous activity she is, for some reason, considered to be inadequate for – such as stirring a barbecue fire. In line with what was found by Belk and Pollay, the vast majority of the themes and settings of these ads portray scenes of modern living that represent aspirational examples of a life of work and consumption. They generally show meaning and a sense of fulfillment that derives from social status, possession and display. Most importantly, they set a script for consumers to learn and strive to reproduce.[24] The educational role of advertising in the postwar times sits in continuation with its pivotal role as a promoter of consumer values in the 1920s and 1930s. Consumer historian Roland Marchand notes that the advertising men of that age considered themselves as pioneers of modernity, the creators of those values that would underpin the affirmation of the modern era in Western society.[25] Ad men in the 1960s – as the series Mad Men vividly recounts – did the same for the masses of consumers that enthusiastically subscribed to a new era of progress.

In particular, the diffusion of the television across the 1950s and 1960s represented a key component in the promotion of the "good life" ideal. Both as an object and a broadcaster of content, the television brought modernity into people's houses, materially as well as symbolically. As media historians underline, the diffusion of the television shrank the perception of the times and spaces of public events, elevating media celebrities to the status of Olympian gods of modernity and role models of the "good life."[26] The powerful relevance of television advertising at the level of the imaginary can still be observed among Baby Boomers, who often reminisce about the TV ads of their childhood. In Italy, for instance, Boomers usually associate kids' bedtime with the broadcast of Carosello – a block of advertisements of all kinds, which aired on Italian state television between 8.30 and 9pm each night between 1957 and 1977. Ask a typical Italian Boomer about Carosello, and they will still have vivid memories, and endless anecdotes, about the most popular ads and characters in it.

What's more, the diffusion of the television did not only contribute to the construction of the imaginary of the "good life," but actually transformed the interior design of households' leisure space – the living room. The trend of furnishing living rooms around a media object dates back a long time, starting from the gramophone in the late 1800s up to, more recently, the radio in the 1930s. Yet in the Baby Boomers era the television affirms as the essential centerpiece of home design, elevated to the status and positioning of a pseudo-cult object, with the rest of the space constructed around it. This has persisted until today to the point that, for many, the absence of a television in one's living room remains an almost unthinkable prospect. One who does not have or, worse, who does not want to have a television in their living room is often seen as either radical, a snob, or "strange." Only now that the youngest generations increasingly make use of streaming services that can be accessed from a smartphone or tablet, instead of watching TV from a television set, this perception is to some extent being crippled.

Alongside advertising, music and particularly vinyl records also played a role in the promotion of the "good life" ideal in the postwar era. The affirmation of pop music in the 1950s and 1960s transformed music into an object that could be collected – the record – and enabled a process of cultural distinction based on the kind of music collected or listened to, that continued for decades. Back then, vinyl records represented the epitome of Ted Ownby's *Dreams of Consumerism,*[27] as objects that represent abundance and novelty. Janet Borgerson and Jonathan Schroeder[28] show how vinyl record covers portrayed vivid snippets of the "good life," being a trove of lifestyle prescriptions and suggestions for aspirational consumption. Just like ads, vinyl covers, they argue, educated postwar consumers to the "good life"; as sketches of modern living, these contributed to the creation of the imaginary of work and consumption that characterized the Boomers era. Only problem: it wasn't meant to last. As Sarah Kendzior notes, Baby Boomers were sold an "unaffordable dream."[29]

The "good life": a generational fracture

Throughout the 1970s and then into the 1980s, following the demise of the 1968 and free love movements, becoming-adult Boomers were afforded a stingy nickname: the "Me Generation." Coined by writer Tom Wolfe in 1976,[30] this label grasps what was perceived as the surge of a culture of self-realization and individualism at the expense of the communitarian ethos incarnated by the hippie generation in the late 1960s. At the same time, this label somewhat anticipates the embrace of the consumer economy by then-adult Boomers in the 1980s, who peaked into their work life adopting a lifestyle that matched the individualist culture of the emergent neoliberal era. This is epitomized in its most glamorous traits by the "yuppies," who colonized cities and their suburbs to live the "good life" of work and consumption in a deeply self-oriented and lavish manner.

It is in this same period that the social pact based on the availability of jobs for life, which was meant to lead to progressive generational prosperity and upwards social mobility for decades to come, begins to decline. Despite their relevance in popular culture and style, the forms of resistance to the ascent of neoliberalism proffered by British subcultures in the late 1970s, such as the punk movement, were soon dismissed as a noisy fad. The rise of Thatcherism in the UK is seen as a conservative reaction to the turmoil of the 1970s, which ultimately scared the older and more established generations as a threat to the social order.[31]

Those who grew up in this period are commonly labeled as Generation X, from the same-name book by Douglas Coupland.[32] Understood as the cohort of people born between the late 1960s and the early 1980s, Generation X came of age in a context where jobs were ceasing to be the structure of certainty toward the "good life." In the increasingly flexible, precarious and "always-on" labor market enabled by neoliberal policies, the pursuit of the "good life" by Gen Xers soon turned into what Janelle Wilson defines as "a generational identity crisis." Wilson writes that, "A sense of doom or pessimism clings to this generation... Generation Xers came of age during the rise of dual-career families, effective birth control, the threat of AIDS, increasing national debt and increasing awareness of the deterioration of the environment. Forty percent of Gen Xers are kids of divorce." Gen X, Wilson argues, is the epitome of the retreat of the American Dream; yet, she continues:

> rather than evoking sympathy, members of Generation X have become a symbol of a society in decline. They are labeled slackers, whiners; the image is of a tuned-out individual, dressed in grunge, not doing a whole lot. Perhaps rather than assuming that Xers are irresponsible, immature, apathetic young adults, we should consider how socio-historical conditions have shaped and affected them.[33]

Popular culture recounts this generational crisis quite dramatically, in two cult books and movies of that time: *Fight Club* and *Trainspotting*. A dark novel written by Chuck Palahniuk and turned into a movie directed by David Fincher, set in a fictional city in the US, *Fight Club* tells the story of Tyler Durden's double personality. At day, he is a soldier of the "good life," who works in a white-collar job and buys Ikea furniture that "matches who he is as a person"; at night, he is the ringleader of a secret fight club and the chief plotter of a paramilitary attack to take down a skyscraper, identified as the symbol of corporate America. In one of his speeches, he solemnly proclaims:

> We're the middle children of history, man. No purpose or place. We have no Great War. No Great Depression. Our Great War's a spiritual war...our Great Depression is our lives. We've all been raised on television to believe that one day we'd all be millionaires, and movie gods, and rock stars. But we won't. And we're slowly learning that fact. And we're very, very pissed off.[34]

Generation X grew up with the promise of living a "good life" that largely failed to materialize. What they got instead was a first-row seat to watch the dismantling of the "good life", propelled by neoliberalism. This engendered alienation and the search for alternatives, as brutally portrayed in *Trainspotting*. Set in Edinburgh, Scotland, *Trainspotting*, a novel written by Irvine Welsh that became a movie directed by Danny Boyle, is the story of a group of drug-addicts and a local alcoholic who struggle to fit into a modern society that wants them to conform to the normative conventions of the "good life," but offers them little else than job centers and benefits. The famous opening monologue of the movie, directed by Danny Boyle and uttered by the lead character, Mark Renton, has the tone of a proper crusade against the "good life" ideal:

> Choose life. Choose a job. Choose a career. Choose a family. Choose a fucking big television. Choose washing machines, cars, compact disc players, and electrical tin openers. Choose good health, low cholesterol and dental insurance. Choose

fixed-interest mortgage repayments. Choose a starter home. Choose your friends. Choose leisure wear and matching luggage. Choose a three-piece suite on hire purchase in a range of fucking fabrics. Choose DIY and wondering who the fuck you are on a Sunday morning. Choose sitting on that couch watching mind-numbing spirit-crushing game shows, stuffing fucking junk food into your mouth. Choose rotting away at the end of it all, pishing your last in a miserable home, nothing more than an embarrassment to the selfish, fucked-up brats you have spawned to replace yourselves. Choose your future. Choose life...But why would I want to do a thing like that? I chose not to choose life: I chose something else. And the reasons? There are no reasons. Who needs reasons when you've got heroin?[35]

In its upsetting unfolding, *Trainspotting* grasps the complex relationship between identity, work and the meaning of life that characterizes Generation X, at the same time digging into the emergent drug-infused club cultures of the late 1980s and early 1990s. Yet, in their crude portraits of Gen X's identity crisis both *Fight Club* and *Trainspotting* are, at least in part, also a complaint of exclusion of Gen X from the "good life," and a stark display of its psychological consequences – in terms of personality disorders for Tyler Durden, or drug abuse for the Trainspotting gang. This is clearly reflected in Wilson's fieldwork interviews, that show how Gen Xers look somewhat nostalgically at the 1950s and 1960s, when Boomers became adult and "everything was possible."[36] Arguably, Generation X experienced a hiatus between their aspirations and the expectations reserved to them by society and by the previous generations, realizing during the process they were sold a lie. See this 1990 *TIME Magazine* article, for instance, which questioned why "twentysomethings" of the time were so skeptical of the Boomers value:

(a)nyone who expected they would echo the boomers who came before, bringing more of the same attitude, should brace for a surprise. This crowd is profoundly different from – even contrary to – the group that came of age in the 1960s and that celebrates itself each week on The Wonder Years and thirtysomething. By and large, the 18-to-29 group scornfully rejects the habits and values of the baby boomers, viewing that group as self-centered, fickle and impractical.[37]

If the 1950s and 1960s were the Golden Age of Capitalism, then the 1990s arguably were the Golden Age of Neoliberalism. The end of the Cold War brought Francis Fukuyama to famously proclaim the definitive affirmation of liberal democracy over socialism as "the end of history"; unemployment figures went down again and a decade of relative prosperity began.[38] This is particularly a tale of the UK, as the end of the divisive Thatcher era led to the affirmation of New Labour and the neoliberal way to the left proposed by Tony Blair – soon to become another burning delusion. Immersed in the imaginary of Cool Britannia, epitomized by Brit Pop sensations Blur and Oasis and by the success of the Young British Artists collective, New Labour branded the UK as the place where art took the lead in society. The imaginary of Cool Britannia vested Blair's ascent to Downing Street, while giving local youth a new sense of hope for the future. Which lasted, again, only for a while.

In the meantime, radical leftist movements against global capitalism blossomed into large-scale protests first in Seattle, 1999 and then Genoa, 2001, where they were tragically repressed by local police. Then, 9/11 led to a revival of American imperialism, 26 years after the Vietnam War, bringing a renewed sentiment of hostility against strangers, particularly Muslims. The honeymoon between Blair and British society came to an abrupt close in 2003, when the UK joined the US in the Iraq war in spite of vehement protests from the public for what was perceived to be an unnecessary military operation. Then, after the boom and bust of the early Internet economy, the financial sector rolled its most dangerous dice: a set of "junk" subprime mortgage titles injected in the system brought to the nationalization of Northern Rock Bank in February 2008, and the collapse of Lehman Brothers in September of the same year. The second Great Recession had arrived. Things will never be the same again.

The demise of the American Dream

Today we live the demise of the American Dream. Dating back to the nineteenth century and the American Declaration of Independence, in the twentieth century and particularly after the two world wars the American Dream came to incarnate the very same imaginary of modernity. Now, at the start of the twenty-first century, the myth that enthused Western societies for decades has turned into a dystopia. Since the 1980s, suggests Lauren Berlant:

> the social democratic promise of the postwar period in the US and Europe has retracted. People have remained attached to unachievable fantasies of the good life – with its promises of upward mobility, job security, political and social equality and durable intimacy – despite evidence that liberal-capitalist societies can no longer be counted on to provide opportunities for individuals to make their lives "add up to something."[39]

Those "people" who have remained attached to unachievable fantasies of the good life, who are now unable to cope with its demise, are first and foremost the Baby Boomers. Growing up at a time of optimism, prosperity and abundance, many of them entertained the notion that subsequent generations would have undoubtedly experienced the same conditions and opportunities they were afforded. This has not happened. On the contrary, the society that Gen Xers and particularly the subsequent cohort, commonly referred to as the Millennials, who are Baby Boomers' children, have grown up into has turned out to be considerably different. Starting from the demise of work as a structure of certainty, up to and including changes in demographics, consumption practices, sexual habits, moral values and lifestyle, for many Baby Boomers today's global, multicultural, politically-correct society is almost unrecognizable from the "simpler" times they grew up in. Thus, they've become the main conveyors of a kind of idealized, "regressive nostalgia" for the society of the postwar era.

We often read that Baby Boomers are to blame for the Brexit and Trump votes. Much of the popular press has no doubt they are: countless articles proclaim that "angry Baby Boomers gave us Brexit and Trump"[40], that Brexit is a "middle finger" to the younger generations[41] or that "Baby Boomers broke America."[42] Academic research shows in fact a more nuanced picture, which suggests to take this assumption with a pinch of salt.[43] Yet, there seems to be some considerable correspondence between the cultural zeitgeist of the Baby Boomers era and the nostalgic calling at the heart of the Brexit and Trump campaigns. To begin with, age and education were arguably significant factors in the Brexit and Trump votes: the Pew Research Centre reports that in the 2016 US election older voters widely preferred Trump over Clinton by an almost 10-point margin. Yet, younger voters did not equally trust Clinton, as she underperformed compared to Obama's success in the younger cohorts in 2012. Concerning education, we can observe a similarly wide gap, with college-educated voters (who are typically younger) being significantly more likely to back Clinton, while those without a college degree (typically older) were significantly more likely to back Trump.[44] For what concerns Brexit, Remain gathered a large chunk of support among the more highly-educated electorate, as opposed to the Leave vote; the latter instead increased with age, and particularly in the 50-64 and 65+ groups, while younger voters opted almost en masse for Remain.[45]

Infused of the Boomers-appealing rhetoric of a return to the societal model of the twentieth century, on the whole the Brexit and Trump votes should be read as a response to the demise of the "good life" ideal of the postwar era. As the political hegemony of the US on the world stage fades out, and other actors – particularly, China and Russia – become prominent, it is now vividly clear in the public perception that the 2007-8 recession is not just a passing malaise of the economy, but the symptom of a systemic shift, that marks the start of a new era. Regressive nostalgia is stronger for older generations precisely because it represents a retaliation for the disintegration of the society that the postwar economic boom, in its peculiar socio-economic unfolding, was able to create.

In the US, this retaliation particularly comes from the inner, rural and suburban lands of America, those often referred to as "flyover country."[46] Take an electoral map of America and you'll see the division. Blue, the color of Democrats, occupies the flanks of the US: California, Oregon, Washington on the Pacific coast, New York, Massachusetts, Maryland on the Atlantic side. Except for some outliers, such as New Mexico and Colorado, the center of the US is Trump Country. Today, Joan Williams argues, America is a case of "class cluelessness": on the one hand, the urban professional class still yields a vision of a middle-class life which is no longer available nor within reach. On the other hand, working-class Americans, instead, particularly in "flyover" countries, feel patronized by the upper middle classes in terms of language, race and manners. For them, a professional life in the knowledge economy is not something to aspire to: technical, manual jobs are authentic and true to their moral values. They see upper middle classes as an elite who played favorites on top of the economic downturn and instead "mandated sympathy for the poor, for people of color, for women, for refugees, for LGBTQ individuals." In "flyover" country, today, working-class women have broadly the same jobs as their mothers, while working-class men don't; the threat against masculine dignity at work among the working classes of Red America is a matter of pride and identity that resonates strongly with the nostalgic calling of the Trump era, especially among the older generations.[47] The same term, "flyover country," is perceived to be a class insult, used to label places you would pass but never stop by, while going somewhere else. For them, "the American Dream is more than having money. It's feeling proud to be an American, and to say 'under God' when you salute the flag, and feel *good* about that. And it's about living in a society that believes in clean, normal family life."[48]

If we look at the UK, we find a similar story. The decade of neoliberal austerity policies that have guided the various Tory (and coalition) governments since 2010 has led to a strain in social security across the country. This has blended with the centripetal force of the capital, London, leaving the heartlands of middle England feeling forgotten and deprived. Thiemo Fetzer, an associate professor at the University of Warwick, evidences how "Leave-supporting areas clearly stand out by being more deprived, having lower levels of income and life satisfaction, less access to high-status jobs, and living in areas with overall weaker economic structure, an aging demographic and lower levels of educational attainment."[49] In other words, provincial areas – not just in the UK and the US, but everywhere in the West – are the cradles of the nostalgic zeitgeist, as the "good life" ideal first colonized them – physically, through large-scale industrialization – and then betrayed them, leaving its ruins behind, made of deindustrialization, dead factories, environmental hazards and mass unemployment. Decades of neoliberal policies, and the staunch belief by left and right politicians that these would have enabled wealth to "trickle down" from the upper echelons of society to everyday folks, which has never actually happened, further aggrieved this sense of disenchantment by non-urban populations.

As argued by George Monbiot, today neoliberalism has finally appeared in its true nature as "the ideology at the root of all our problems."[50] Perhaps the great masterpiece of neoliberalism has been to operate a gentrification not just of cities and inlands, but of class relations. As Owen Jones notes in *Chavs*, the neoliberal ideal is that we have *all* become middle class now.[51] The neoliberal ideology does not see class stratification: it sees, instead, different kinds of effort applied by individuals in succeeding in life, with varying results, irrespective of pre-existing capitals and resources. As an ideology of meritocracy, neoliberalism blatantly ignores the barriers to success that individuals in fact encounter in pursuing their life plans as a consequence of where they come from, and the constraints they face. Decades of neoliberal rhetoric ultimately anesthetized the perception of how relevant class background is in society, making class relations invisible to many. The 2007-8 crash, which brought a new spike in economic inequality,[52] made the unequal allocation of resources in society visible again, so that the working classes began to realize what had actually happened. Nostalgic populist fantasies, sold by ruthless politicians in a context of opinion polarization and algorithmic public spheres, provided the easiest shortcut to navigate this complexity.

* * *

In short: work, and changes in the role of work as the baseline for living a "good life," are where to find the seeds of the nostalgic zeitgeist of the start of the twenty-first century. For those who grew up in the belief of the "good life" ideal, notes Lauren Berlant, work has turned into a "fantasy of meritocracy" and "a story about plenitude and scarcity – about so many bad jobs available to so many contingent workers and never enough money, never enough love, and barely any rest." Nostalgia is the inevitable end result of the collapse of the twentieth century ideal of the "good life," as nostalgia incarnates "(t)he desire for a less-bad life" that "involves finding resting places," a rest that is "imagined nostalgically...in the places where rest is supposed to have happened." The fantasy of the "good life", Berlant concludes, thus becomes a "desperate regression toward the desire to soon experience an imaginary security one *knows* without having ever had."[53]

If this is the imaginary within which Baby Boomers and Gen X have respectively grown up, one may wonder what is instead the cultural imaginary that characterizes today's younger generations, those we referred to earlier as Millennials, those who came of age after 9/11 and began their work life in coincidence with the 2007-8 crash. It looks as though Millennials strive to build their own "good life" ideal. Ironically, however, some of them in order to do so also look *back* – yet, in a very, very different way.

Notes

[1] GOV.UK, *Demographic, diversity and socioeconomic profile of Havering's population*, 2014, p. 24. Available at: https://www3. havering.gov.uk/Documents/Equality-and-Diversity/ Appendix%202_Demographic,%20Diversity%20and%20 Socio-economic%20Profile%20of%20Havering's%20 Population%20Jan-13.pdf (Last accessed 24 July 2019).

[2] See Sasha O. Becker, Thiemo Fetzer and Dennis Novy, "Who voted for Brexit? A comprehensive district-level analysis." *Economic Policy*, 2017, 32(92), pp. 601-650; Matthew Goodwin and Caitlin Milazzo, "Taking back control? Investigating the role of immigration in the 2016 vote for Brexit." *The British Journal of Politics and International Relations*, 2017, 19(3), pp. 450-64.

[3] Zygmunt Bauman, *Retrotopia*. London: Polity, 2017, p. 60.

[4] "Horrible spike" in hate crime linked to Brexit vote, Met police say," *Guardian*, 2017. Available at: https://www. theguardian.com/society/2016/sep/28/hate-crime-horrible-spike-brexit-vote-metropolitan-police (Last accessed 12 April 2019).

[5] "The slow-burning hatred that led Thomas Mair to murder Jo Cox," *Guardian*, 2016. Available at: https://www. theguardian.com/uk-news/2016/nov/23/thomas-mair-slow-burning-hatred-led-to-jo-cox-murder (Last accessed 12 April 2019).

[6] John Harris, "If you've got money, you vote in…if you haven't got money, you vote out," *Guardian*, 2016. Available at: https:// www.theguardian.com/politics/commentisfree/2016/jun/24/ divided-britain-brexit-money-class-inequality-westminster (Last accessed 26 April 2019).

[7] "Trump on Charlottesville: 'I think there's blame on both sides,'" *CBS*, 2017. Available at: https://www.cbsnews.com/ news/trump-on-charlottesville-i-think-theres-blame-on-both-sides/ (Last accessed 12 April 2019).

[8] "Full transcript: Donald Trump's jobs plan speech," *Politico*, 2016. Available at: https://www.politico.com/story/2016/06/ full-transcript-trump-job-plan-speech-224891 (Last accessed 26 April 2019).

[9] Joan C. Williams, J. C., *White working class: overcoming class cluelessness in America*. Cambridge, Mass: Harvard Business Press, 2017.

[10] See C. Wright Mills, *White collar; the American middle classes*, New York, 1951, and "Read: Obama's Speech on the Middle Class," *The Atlantic*, 2013. Available at: https://www. theatlantic.com/politics/archive/2013/07/read-obamas-speech-middle-class/312948/ (Last accessed 26 April 2019).

[11] Emil Westacott, "What does it mean to live the 'good life?',," 2019. Available at: https://www.thoughtco.com/what-is-the-good-life-4038226 (last accessed 12 April 2019); Hartmut

Rosa, "

[12] Lauren Berlant, *Cruel optimism*. Durham: Duke University Press, 2017.

[13] Lizabeth Cohen, "A consumers' republic: the politics of mass consumption in postwar America." *Journal of Consumer Research*, 2004, 31(1), pp. 236-9.

[14] Doug Owram, *Born at the right time: A history of the baby-boom generation*. Toronto: University of Toronto Press, 1997.

[15] Sandra L. Colby and Jennifer M. Ortman, J. M, "The baby boom cohort in the United States: 2012 to 2060." *US Census Bureau*, 2014.

[16] See for instance Alan France and Steven Roberts, "The problem of social generations: a critique of the new emerging orthodoxy in youth studies." *Journal of Youth Studies*, 2015, 18(2), pp. 215-30; David Costanza, "Can we please stop talking about generations as if they are a thing?" *Slate*, 2018. Available at: https://amp.slate.com/technology/2018/04/the-evidence-behind-generations-is-lacking.html (Last accessed 24 July 2019).

[17] Monika Krause, "What is Zeitgeist? Examining period-specific cultural patterns." *Poetics*, 2019, p. 1, [online], available at: https://doi.org/10.1016/j.poetic.2019.02.003.

[18] Janelle L. Wilson, *Nostalgia: sanctuary of meaning*. Lewisburg, PA: Bucknell University Press, 2005, p. 89.

[19] Robert D. Putnam, *Our kids: The American dream in crisis*. New York: Simon and Schuster, 2016.

[20] "Occupational Employment Statistics, 1960-70." *Bureau of Labor Statistics*, 1972. Available at: https://eric.ed.gov/?id=ED073294 (Last accessed 26 April 2019).

[21] Daniel Bell, "The impact of advertising," *New Leader* 6 (1957): 9-11, as cited in Russell W. Belk, Richard W. Pollay, "Images of ourselves: The good life in twentieth century advertising." *Journal of Consumer Research*, 1985, 11(4), pp. 887-97.

[22] Christopher Lasch, *The Culture of Narcissism: American Life in an age of diminishing expectations*. W.W. Norton & Company, 1991; Russell W. Belk, Richard W. Pollay, "Images of ourselves: the good life in twentieth century advertising." *Journal of Consumer Research*, 1985, 11(4), pp. 887-97.

[23] Jim Heimann, *All-American Ads 60s*, Taschen, 2003.

[24] Roland Marchand, *Advertising the American dream: making way for modernity, 1920-1940*. Univ of California Press, 1985. See also: Darren Garrett, "How ad men invented the future," Medium, 2018. Available at: https://howwegettonext. com/how-ad-men-invented-the-future-cf3f81139c08 (Last accessed 24 July 2019).

[25] Edgar Morin, *L'esprit du temps*. Paris, Grasset, 1962.

[26] Janelle L. Wilson, *Nostalgia: sanctuary of meaning*. Lewisburg, PA: Bucknell University Press, 2005.

[27] Ted Ownby, *American dreams in Mississippi: consumers, poverty, & culture, 1830-1998*. University of North Carolina Press, 1999.

[28] Janet Borgerson, J.E, Schroeder, *Designed for hi-fi living: the vinyl LP in midcentury America*. Cambridge, Mass: MIT Press, 2017.

[29] Sarah Kendzior, *The view from flyover country: dispatches from the forgotten America*. Flatiron Books, 2018, p. 68.

[30] Tom Wolfe, "The 'me' decade and the third great awakening." *New York Magazine*, 1976. Available at: http:// nymag.com/news/features/45938/ (Last accessed 26 April 2019).

[31] On the rise of Thatcherism, see Stuart Hall, "The great moving right show." *Marxism Today*, 1979, 23(1), pp. 14-20.

[32] Douglas Coupland, *Generation X: Tales for an accelerated culture*. New York: Macmillan, 1991.

[33] Janelle L. Wilson, *Nostalgia: Sanctuary of Meaning*. Lewisburg, PA: Bucknell University Press, 2005, pp. 91-2.

[34] Chuck Palahniuk, *Fight Club: a novel*. W.W. Norton &

Company, 2005, p. 78.

[35] Trainspotting, directed by Danny Boyle, 1996. Adapted from Irvine Welsh, *Trainspotting*. Secker and Warburg, 1993.

[36] Janelle L. Wilson, *Nostalgia: sanctuary of meaning*. Lewisburg, PA: Bucknell University Press, 2005, pp. 93-104.

[37] See: "Living: proceeding with caution," *Time*, 2019. Available at: http://content.time.com/time/subscriber/ article/0,33009,970634-1,00.html (Last accessed 26 April 2019); Jason Wilson, "Gen X has survived its gloomy formative years. Now we will have to deal with climate change," *Guardian*, 2019. Available at: https://www. theguardian.com/environment/commentisfree/2019/feb/21/ gen-x-has-survived-its-gloomy-formative-years-now-we-will-have-to-deal-with-climate-change (Last accessed 24 July 2019).

[38] See Fukuyama, F. (1989). "The end of history?" *The National Interest*, (16), 3-18; Marcus, M. (2002) *A Graphic Overview of Employment and Earnings in the 1990s*, available at: http://www.ibrc.indiana.edu/ibr/2002/fall02/pdfs/3_employment. pdf (Last accessed 26 April 2019).

[39] Lauren Berlant, *Cruel optimism*. Durham: Duke University Press, 2011, back cover.

[40] "Why angry baby boomers gave us Trump and now, Brexit," *Forbes*, 2016. Available at: https://www.forbes.com/sites/ johnmcquaid/2016/06/30/why-angry-baby-boomers-gave-us-trump-and-now-brexit/#5c10de85c5d2 (Last accessed 26 April 2019).

[41] "Brexit is a middle finger from the baby boomers to young people like me," *Vox*, 2016. Available at: https://www.vox. com/2016/6/24/12025954/brexit-young-voters-remain (Last accessed 26 April 2019).

[42] "How baby boomers broke America," *Time*, 2018. Available at: http://time.com/5280446/baby-boomer-generation-america-steve-brill/ (Last accessed 26 April 2019).

[43] Kieran Devine, "Not all the 'over 65s' are in favour of Brexit – Britain's wartime generation are almost as pro-EU as millennials," *LSE Blogs*, 2019. Available at: https://blogs.lse.ac.uk/europpblog/2019/03/21/not-all-the-over-65s-are-in-favour-of-brexit-britains-wartime-generation-are-almost-as-pro-eu-as-millennials/; Jennie Bristow, "How did baby boomers get the blame for Brexit?" *LSE Blogs*, 2017. Available at: https://blogs.lse.ac.uk/brexit/2017/02/20/how-did-baby-boomers-get-the-blame-for-brexit/ (Last accessed 26 April 2019).

[44] "Behind Trump's victory: divisions by race, gender, education," *Pew Research Centre*, 2016. Available at: https://www.pewresearch.org/fact-tank/2016/11/09/behind-trumps-victory-divisions-by-race-gender-education/ (Last accessed 26 April 2019).

[45] How Brexit vote broke down, *POLITICO*, 2016. Available at: https://www.politico.eu/article/graphics-how-the-uk-voted-eu-referendum-brexit-demographics-age-education-party-london-final-results/ (Last accessed 26 April 2019).

[46] Sarah Kendzior, *The view from flyover country: dispatches from the forgotten America*. Flatiron Books, 2018.

[47] Joan C. Williams, *White working class: overcoming class cluelessness in America*. Cambridge, Mass: Harvard Business Press, 2017, p. 12.

[48] Arlie R. Hochschild, *Strangers in their own land: anger and mourning on the American right*. New York: The New Press, 2018, p. 165, as cited in Williams, 2017.

[49] Thiemo Fetzer, *Austerity swung voters to Brexit – and now they are changing their minds*, LSE Blogs, 2018. Available at: https://blogs.lse.ac.uk/brexit/2018/11/19/austerity-swung-voters-to-brexit-and-now-they-are-changing-their-minds/ (Last accessed 26 April 2019).

[50] George Monbiot, "Neoliberalism – the ideology at the root of all our problems," *Guardian*, 2016. Available at: https://

www.theguardian.com/books/2016/apr/15/neoliberalism-ideology-problem-george-monbiot (Last accessed 26 April 2019).

[51] Owen Jones, *Chavs: the demonization of the working class*. London: Verso, 2012.

[52] Thomas Piketty, *Capital in the 21st century*. Trans. Arthur Goldhammer. Belknap Press, 2014.

[53] Lauren Berlant, *Cruel optimism*. Durham: Duke University Press, 2011, p. 167 and p. 180.

3. Hipsters (will save the world)

Rent a flat above a shop
Cut your hair and get a job
Smoke some fags and play some pool
Pretend you never went to school
But still you'll never get it right
'cos when you're laying in bed at night
Watching roaches climb the wall
If you called your dad he could stop it all
Pulp, Common People

East London. If you ask a random bunch of twentysomethings whether they consider themselves "hipsters', they'll almost certainly deny with disdain. No one really seems to be happy to be identified as a hipster. Go to Paris's XI arrondissement, or Williamsburg in New York, to Kreuzberg in Berlin, to Isola or Navigli in Milan, and you'll get similar answers. And yet: everybody will know what you're talking about. What's more: these places all look very similar to each other. Why?

* * *

Hipster culture is a landmark phenomenon of the start of the twenty-first century, particularly (albeit not solely) in the Western world. The term "hipster" dates back to the 1940s, when it was used in the US to identify jazz music fans, usually white, who sought to imitate the style and music taste of black youth. Today, we typically call "hipsters" those 20- to 35-year-old middle-class "urban bohemians" who work in the creative industries and/or in cafés, bars or retail, and live in postindustrial gentrified areas where factories have been left abandoned, and the housing market is more affordable.[1] As a style, hipster culture represents an evolution of the indie subculture of the late 1990s, which promoted a (bland) counter-movement against practices of industrialization in fashion, music and creativity, in favor of "independent" and "authentic" forms of consumption and production. Over the years, this grew on to become a mainstream and clearly-defined aesthetics. Its stereotypical markers are: a curated beard and/or a funky mustache for boys, 1950s hair (sometimes with a fringe) for girls; nerdy glasses; lumberjack-checked flannel shirts and striped t-shirts; trousers that are either too comfy or too skinny, usually rolled up at the ankle. Often made object of mockery, the hipster look is an eclectic mix of vintage, colorful items inspired by (or directly taken from) fashion trends of the past, particularly the 1980s, usually bought at charity shops, vintage markets, independent stores or cheap fast fashion chains that sell disposable but "organic" clothes, all patched together in a rather varied style.[2] Many laugh at them, with a bit of that typically bourgeois sense of entitlement that urban middle classes sometimes cannot resist to display. But, as they say: there's more to the picture than meets the eye.

Walking through these neighborhoods, in fact, something actually stands out. Places like Williamsburg, Shoreditch and Kreuzberg are highly multicultural areas where natives and immigrants, blacks and whites, Western and Eastern, queer and straight humanity all coexist together, for the most part peacefully and in harmony. Those less happy are sometimes the older inhabitants of these districts, who have seen the places they've lived in for decades rapidly change as a consequence of ruthless gentrification processes that have often been tough to digest, considering how quickly they've unfolded. Still, despite issues that exist, older folks have ultimately accepted the newly "hip" status of their neighborhoods, blending in with a young and diverse population and the changes they brought to these areas.

What's more, these districts are characterized by a conspicuous presence of those independent shops and boutiques, vintage and second-hand markets, art studios and shared workspaces, that make them the capitals of coolness of the Western world. Look around: coffee houses that serve expensive, sophisticated brews; barbershops trimming hair in 1930s fashion; bars with vintage decor and neon lights that experiment with refined drinks; "natural wine" restaurants and craft beer pubs. Over the last decades, these turned from being niche consumption trends to an actually mainstream set of practices which, despite their apparent heterogeneity, are ultimately connoted by a common imaginary. This may be seen as characterized by a kind of "progressive" nostalgia, that looks *back* at practices of production and consumption from a pre-capitalist world and, in so doing, promotes an alternative to the modes of producing and consuming of the decaying industrial order. What if hipsters, after all, are the pioneers of a new "good life" ideal, in the demise of the old one? Let's take them seriously, for once.

Marginal distinction

Milan is a textbook example of "hipsterization". The classic design of Milanese buildings and streets, with their elegance and structure, blends with the aesthetics of the new hipster high street, made of independent boutiques and food venues, that restyled entire neighborhoods over the last decade, particularly in coincidence with the 2015 Expo. Walk through Navigli – the traditional "hip" quarter of the city – and you'll see a variety of local and global food trends on display, in a blossoming of cheap and less cheap options. There, Apulian's "puccia" (a stuffed-up focaccia sandwich) and Neapolitan pizza places sit side-by-side with Hawaiian poké and traditional aperitivo bars, expensive sushi restaurants and gourmet burger grills, being hotspots for local youth and tourists alike. Similar landscapes can be observed in the more recently hip areas of Isola and NoLo, once industrial areas characterized by high immigration from the south of Italy and, later, from developing countries, that have recently gained newfound popularity for their (relatively) cheaper accommodation costs and their cool nightlife scene. NoLo, in particular, which stands for "North of Loreto," a Milanese variation of Soho's "South of Houston" acronym, is an increasingly popular and debated one, due to the rapid gentrification process it has experienced in the last few years, as it went from being a rundown, almost neglected suburb to become the epitome of the Milanese alternative scene, subject to brutal real estate speculation.

Food and food taste are among the key playgrounds of hipster culture. In a 2010 essay written for the *New York Times*, Mark Grief underlines how hipsters use taste as their "primary currency." Hipsters, Grief argues, "play at being the inventors or first adopters of novelties: pride comes from knowing, and deciding, what's cool in advance of the rest of the world." In a same-year piece that appeared on *Nymag*, Grief underlines that hipsters are quintessentially about "superior knowledge" of trends "before anyone else."[3] While this is admittedly true, I would argue such a reading improperly reduces hipsters' taste-making negotiations to an individualist, elitist and snobbish practice. The quest for being in-the-know that is typical of hipster cultures, instead, actually hides a more complex social dynamic.

On the whole, hipsters demographically overlap with what we identified earlier as the highly-educated and precarity-afflicted Millennials generation. Hipster culture in other words emerges as a prominent social phenomenon at a moment in history when the prescriptive model of upwards social mobility that established in the twentieth century, based on work as a conduit to mass consumption, had become inaccessible to many and unable to reproduce itself on a large scale. As a fraction of the Millennials generation, hipsters therefore should be seen on the whole as a social group characterized by the possession of comparatively high cultural capital and comparatively low economic capital. Hence, I would argue the rise of hipster culture and its emphasis on taste negotiations – within and beyond food cultures – represent a way by part of the Millennials generation to vindicate their marginalized social and economic condition. Put differently, the frenzy about authenticity and being in-the-know by hipsters is not just a superficial practice or a futile social game. On the contrary, it is a way to, using Bourdieusian jargon, reaffirm their otherwise unspent cultural capital by means of sophisticated consumer choices, seen as a conduit to acquiring that social status which is not given to them by an established occupational condition.

I call this a process of "marginal distinction," intended in two main ways. On the one hand, echoing the economics notion of marginal utility, it may be argued that the hipsters' quest for being in-the-know entails, *à la Grief*, that the more a particular taste becomes incrementally popular, the less it carries social gain – a process epitomized by the expression "before it was cool." On the other hand, however, it also entails the peculiar capacity to grasp the tiny little differences that set two similar products apart and be able to decode them. "Marginal," in this second nuance, means therefore the "liminal" valorization of one's cultural capital, which can be found in the capacity to detect and recognize an unknown, uncommon or particularly refined taste. In this sense, organic coffee is coffee, *just a tiny bit different*; craft beer is beer, *just a tiny bit different*. Put differently, for hipsters it is not just a matter of *knowing of* something before others do; more accurately, it is about *being capable of knowing* the differences between certain products, tastes or items, and playing them out as a conduit to social status.

Consumer research has highlighted the diffusion of new modes of consumption in late modernity, characterized by what has been described as "emerging cultural capital." This is considered a form of cultural capital peculiar to younger, high-educated consumers, constituted by a "heterarchy" of modes of cultural appreciation that is argued to have the potential to reshape the content of elite culture in the years to come.[4] Among these forms of "emerging cultural capital" can be located the modes of consumption peculiar to hipster culture, particularly the preference for niche, craft, artisanal, independently-produced, "authentic" goods. In a research on craft beer aficionados, Andre Maciel and Melanie Wallendorf identify how participants in craft beer tasting circles employ practices of "taste engineering" based on a nuanced notion of cultural competence, that is principled on "the ability to detect the flavors that are indicative of a particular beer style." This is not merely a reaction to mainstream taste, but has the goal of achieving cultural competence, seeking for diversity and experience. This creates new codes and cultural conventions that acquire value once recognized by others in the scene. Actors in this scene, Maciel and Wallendorf conclude, "derive more prestige by sharing a repertoire of understandings, rules, and engagements with others," and engage in forms of sociality that are not exclusionary toward those less competent, but rather communitarian "interconsumer collaborative practices."[5]

Put differently, hipster culture may be seen as epitomous of a larger process of repurposing the relationship between class and social status that Giana Eckhardt and Fleura Bardhi describe as typical of late modernity, and of which "culture creatives" are conveyors of.[6] Grasping marginal taste differences, I argue, is the device through which participants in hipster culture construct and agree upon new conventions that are conducive to the acquisition and display of social status *without* leaning on the possession of a middle-class job as a conduit to social recognition. In this context, nostalgia – in the form of cultural valorization of old, sometimes pre-industrial practices and modes of production – plays a key role, as it represents the cultural imaginary that underpins the unfolding of these new conventions as well as the repository of cultural references which hipsters pick from to exercise marginal distinction. Nostalgia, in other words, is a precondition to the overall process of marginal distinction as status-seeking practice in hipster culture.

This, of course, does not go without contradictions. Arguably, in order to be acquainted with marginal tastes one must actually be able to afford access to relatively expensive practices, as organic coffee or gourmet burgers usually cost more than their industrial counterparts. An upper- or middle-class background, inevitably, remains a good predictor of the possibility to afford a hipster lifestyle. Furthermore, as said, the emergence of "hip" neighborhoods is accompanied by harsh gentrification processes, which drive house rental costs up and lead to the displacement and impoverishment of working-class folks and ethnic minorities. The affirmation of Airbnb further intensifies this process, as the "hip" status of these neighborhoods ensures the presence of a thriving market of short rentals which further undermines the fabric of the local community.[7]

And yet: it may be argued that marginal distinction practices and their nostalgic imaginary matter because they are not just a consumption fad, but a script and a cultural model that designs a new ideal for a living. This entails a more ethical way of consuming and producing, setting the stage for a broader ethical shift in the values that underpin the meeting of work and consumption in society. In fact, marginal distinction processes do not simply restyle symbolic boundaries of coolness for consumers but represent a key component in the processes of valorization of how a product is made, that henceforth reflect in production practices and the kind of work these involve. What's more, marginal distinction processes are what attracts highly-educated middle-class kids who could not, or did not want to, access the knowledge economy, to newly-cool working-class jobs in the craft industries.

"Retrofuturism"

To witness how this is not just abstract sociological thinking, but actually matches the reality on the ground, meet Aurora. A 33-year-old "hip" baker in Milan, after a degree in chemistry Aurora decided to stay away from the pharmaceutical industry to instead research how to cook bread "the old way," experimenting with sourdough and working to recuperate baking traditions that were partly lost as a result of industrialization. Today, after working at a few established bakeries, including a brief work experience in East London, she is the proud owner of a small business, *Le Polveri*, literally "the powders," housed in a tiny little space just minutes away from Navigli. Her bakery is regularly featured in mainstream magazines and in the specialized press as a successful example of food innovation and female entrepreneurship.

As she tells me about the path to setting up her own business, I'm struck by a reference to the generational distance that she feels between the idea of work held by her parents' cohort – former Boomers – and that of people her age. Compared to 30 or 40 years ago, she says, today work is no longer a certainty but something one must build from scratch – just like her bread. It is difficult for older generations to understand this evolution, she argues, and it is even more difficult for them to accept that in a state of institutionalized uncertainty one would rather prefer to spend time doing something s/he feels passionate for, rather than just looking for a source of income, whatever that is. For her, the fatigue of manually working the dough is where she finds meaning in her work: to accept the fatigue of the baker's work, with one's brain and body, she says, is her "good life."

While our conversation shifts toward what makes her bread so special, she tells me that much of what she has learned about baking is thanks to a bread master she used to work for, Davide Longoni, a pioneer in using ancient grains in Milan. Longoni describes his baking philosophy as "retrofuturism":

going back to go forward. Aurora sees herself following in Longoni's footsteps. Industrialization processes have deprived us of the knowledge of what bread actually represents, she argues. Because of supermarket bread, we are now accustomed to thinking of bread as a one-portion item, she explains, while working the dough in front of me. Instead, she notes, before industrialization and supermarkets bread used to be a bigger loaf, that was meant to be sliced and shared communally. We need to recuperate bread sharing as a communal practice, she notes, underlining that "hip" food-related endeavors like hers are not actually just about putting a product on the market and making it cool in order to sell. They are, on the contrary, about promoting a culture of consuming food that is alternative to industrialization, which is no longer sustainable or desirable. Going back to old and small-scale production practices, she concludes, is not just branding: it is a necessity and the only progressive way to the future.

Another example of this new kind of interlocking relationship between work, production and consumption is the "natural wine" movement. A kind of subculture in the wine world, the natural wine movement is made of producers and consumers who stay away from industrial practices of winemaking and actually look *back* to production techniques that pre-date industrialization and exclude the addition of chemical components to the produce. Often overlapping with other winemaking practices, such as biodynamic or organic wine, the "natural" label indicates that producers of this kind of wine refrain from making use of additives, pesticides and non-natural sulfites in the production process. This allows the production of wines that regularly differ from one year to another and are henceforth made the object of a cult following by a community of connoisseurs, which is rapidly expanding worldwide, who appreciate their unstandardized, raw and "funky" taste. Natural wine in other words is wine, but *just a tiny bit different.*

Xabier Alvarez-Valdes, the owner and head chef of Trangallan, a "gastrocultural" restaurant in Newington Green, north-east London, one of the coolest hotspots for natural wine in the city, tells me that the natural wine movement is first and foremost about "opposing the homogenization of wine created by the wine industry, and recuperating the individuality of wine." Industrial processes, he continues, have taken wine away from what it was originally, making it a commodity like any other. Go to the supermarket, he says, and you will find what he describes as "Coca Cola wine": it all tastes the same. Natural wine, instead, is about valorizing the peculiar features of regional terroirs and the tiny little differences among them, not just in the soil but also in the slope and exposure of a single vineyard. Producers and operators in the natural wine world see themselves not merely as preservers of wine heritage – "the resistance," as Xabi tells me they call themselves – but as a communitarian culture that actually promotes a fairer and progressive way to winemaking, somewhat akin to a creative economy, in which value resides in the authenticity of the produce. The culture that is core to the production of natural wine is reflected in a thriving hospitality scene, with cities like London, Paris and Copenhagen hosting an increasing number of restaurants and bars that stock natural wine, many of which become cult venues and tourist destinations. Those who work at these restaurants as waiters or chefs are often also either natural wine makers themselves, or otherwise deeply engaged in the wider community, attending harvests or natural wine fairs. Their job, in other words, is not just another low-skilled occupation but one where meaning comes from the participation in an emergent cultural practice, that requires competence and a rather sophisticated, "marginal" taste.

The story of the natural wine movement is exemplary of the changing relationship between low-skilled work and high cultural capital that is brilliantly narrated by sociologist Richard

Ocejo in the book *Masters of Craft*. Discussing about the meaning of craft work for craft workers themselves, Ocejo recounts how cocktail makers in hipster bars find meaning in their job when they meet customers who are open to experiment with their choices, and therefore ask bartenders to "do what they want" with their cocktails instead of imposing their pre-existing taste upon them. Using this and other examples, Ocejo shows how middle-class youth in the twenty-first century has turned to low-skilled occupation in craft economies to practice "authentic," meaningful work, that entails the possession, acquisition and display of "emergent cultural capital." In the context of a twenty-first century knowledge economy that is unable to absorb much of the highly-skilled supply of work, sectors such as the hospitality and food industry have become an attractive (sometimes, the only) option for many in search of a career that is not just made of "any job" but that actually fulfills aspirations of meaning. The resurgence of old trades such as barbering, bartending, distilling and butchering that Ocejo describes can be explained, he argues, precisely by the authenticity offered by jobs that are traditionally considered low-skilled or manual occupations – yet repackaged with the nostalgic framework of coolness that is typical of hipster culture.[8]

Food economies, eventually, are where this is most visible. Another sociologist, Chris Land, describes these as "neo-craft industries." These, Land writes:

combine a traditional craft imaginary, concerned with the skillful production of high-quality products, with innovation in both product and process. Craft brewing provides a good example. More than 1,000 new breweries opened in the UK between 2012 and 2017 – an increase of more than 60 percent. By the end of 2017 there were over 6,000 craft breweries in the USA, accounting for 23 percent of the total beer market, though with some evidence of slowing growth.

"Operating at a smaller scale than giants like AB InBev or MillerCoors," Land continues, "these brewers offer a less industrialized organization of production, combining an integrated labor process with innovation in terms of beer styles, ingredients, strengths and brewing techniques." This, Land suggests, is exemplary of a nostalgic calling typical of craft cultures, the nature of which is ultimately not conservative, but progressive: while craft, Land writes, "would appear to hark back to a golden age of meaningful work predating task-fragmentation and industrialization, the small-scale production and ceaseless innovation suggests more of a post-industrial imaginary."[9]

A new "good life?"

At this point, it has hopefully become sufficiently clear that when we talk about hipsters, we should dismiss the stereotypical picture of a bearded man in a flannel shirt, and actually take what they do seriously. The heterogeneous, sometimes contradictory ensemble of practices that sit under the hipster umbrella actually represent a vivid portrait of the post-middle class condition of the Millennials generation.

Usually identified as the cohort born between 1980 and 1993, Western Millennials grew up in the 1990s, the older segments coming of age in the early 2000s, filled with the expectations and assumptions about work and the "good life" held by their Boomer parents. Get a degree, then "cut your hair and get a job," paraphrasing Jarvis Cocker: this is what many of them were told. *Any job.* The safest, the better, ideally in the public administration or at a bank, whose role as an employer is often mythologized by Boomers: "How can you say no to a job at a bank?" they say, since a job at a bank alludes to certainty and a rock-solid pathway to the good life. *If only.*

After decades of neoliberal policies and, in part, also as a direct consequence of the 2007 crash, Millennials in the West have been largely denied access to the lifestyle that much of the Baby Boomer generation enjoyed. Their pursuit of the "good life" has been, instead, much more like a winding road. A 2019 study by the Pew Research Centre on the economic condition of Millennials in American society shows that, on the whole, Millennials are significantly worse off in terms of income if compared to what Boomers earned at the same age. Those with a college education are more or less catching up with Generation X in terms of income generation, but overall Millennials are less likely to be homeowners and remain instead heavy renters, they delay or forego marriage and live (or have lived) at their parents' house much longer than previous cohorts.[10]

Many Western Millennials actually did strive, and somewhat manage, to live the "good life" of work and consumption their parents enjoyed. They got a job and married around 30, often in church (often without actually being religious at all: trends show they are the less religious generation of all);[11] they bought a house, had kids and actually succeeded in replicating the model of capitalist living that the twentieth century society prescribed. By and large, those who made it think about themselves as the norm that should be followed by all. Yet if they look around, they are more like the exception. Many others in fact did not "cut their hair and get a job." Instead, they took their passports and left – by desire or, more frequently, by necessity. This trend is particularly significant for Mediterranean countries, which have seen many young kids leave for places that are perceived to be more open and rich of opportunities, such as the UK (remember, Brexit?). One example: between 2007 and 2017, the number of Italians who left the country in search of a better future tripled.[12] Many of them are nostalgic, in the truest sense, of what they left behind. Class background, again, significantly matters here, as a more comfortable economic condition is often what allows these young people to move in the first place, as they can benefit from the "parachute generation" of their Boomer parents to cover up for their precarious financial situations.

Yet, much like Baby Boomers and Generation X, as a cohort Millennials have been regularly misrepresented in the press, in favor of cheap generalizations. Interestingly, some of the assumptions that characterize Millennials are reformulations of older tropes. One is the myth of entitlement: Millennials have been described as the "Me Me Me generation," a selfish bunch of lazy kids immersed in computers – and, later, smartphones – who are largely uninterested in what surrounds them. In the workplace, they are stereotypically considered to be striving for independence while resisting to hierarchies and fixed rules. They want flexibility and seek to pursue their own interests above all else.[13] But is it true?

James Cairns, an associate professor at Wilfried Laurel University, in Canada, argues this is not the case. Cairns debunks the myth of entitlement attached to Millennials, stating that this serves the (not so) vested interest of the older generations in maintaining a status quo that remains vastly unbalanced in their favor. Instead, Cairns notes, Millennials should be seen more appropriately as "generation screwed."[14] Data confirm this uncharitable picture: in the EU area, for instance, the overall unemployment rate grew by 6.8 percent between the second quarter of 2008 and mid-2010, when many Millennials first entered the job market, reaching the "record level" number of 26.5 million unemployed in the second quarter of 2013.[15] Youth unemployment rates spiked in the same period, going from 15.1 percent in the first quarter of 2008 to 23.9 percent in the first quarter of 2013.[16] In short, by the time Millennials went into the world, the structures of certainty the previous generations had constructed were gone. For Millennials, the world their predecessors created – a society based on work – is no longer an option.

What's more, in the Angloamerican world many Millennials are plagued by a huge education debt. Sarah Kendzior recounts that "(i)n 1968, $2,545 was about the most you could expect to pay for college – most schools cost half as much, and many public universities were still free." Then, she continues, students "graduated with little to no debt, unlike today's university graduate, who owes an average of $27000." This is just one example of the extent to which things have changed for a young adult from the 1960s to the new century. Many Millennials are actually employed in insecure contracts and have to undertake work for free in order to establish professionally at the beginning of their careers, an option that is available only to those who can afford to live without being paid for an extensive period of time. A recent OECD report estimates that only less than six out of ten Millennials in the US can be considered "middle class."[17]

And yet: Millennials are now the second-largest generation in the US electorate, after Boomers. As a cohort, they are more ethnically diverse and generally better educated than previous generations.[18] How do they see the future, and who do they vote for? So far, Millennials look rather disengaged from politics, and their election turnout remains substantially low. In the 2016 US election, a majority of Millennials voted in favor of Hillary Clinton, but only slightly, with higher percentages scored among women and high-educated voters. Perhaps not entirely unsurprisingly, Trump outperformed Clinton among white, less educated Millennials. [19] A similar trend can be observed in Italy in the 2019 EU elections, when a majority of Millennials voted for the far-right League party and for its leader Matteo Salvini.[20] In the Brexit referendum, while in terms of votes they largely favored Remain, Millennials have been blamed for low voter turnout.[21] As the aforementioned Pew Research study concludes, the political potential of Millennials remains largely unfulfilled.[22] It is also true, however, that few Millennials have run for the highest levels of public office yet. But many more will soon, as exemplified by emergent figures such as Alexandria Ocasio-Cortez and Pete Buttigieg, who are considered as rising stars in the US Democratic camp. We'll see if the presence of Millennial representatives in mainstream politics will affect their electoral participation or otherwise produce significant changes in their voting habits.

In the meantime, as the environmental, cultural and practical demise of the societal model based on full-time work and mass consumption in an industrial society finally becomes apparent, Millennials must come to terms with a challenging scenario. Alongside hipster cultures, a growing portion of Millennials seems to be actually interested in promoting a more sustainable way of living, made of practices of waste recycling, deindustrialized and small-scale production and more conscientious consumption, particularly, again, in the food industry. The broad popularity of trends such as vegetarianism, pescetarianism and veganism among Millennials, as well as their widespread embrace of initiatives to raise awareness around climate change, are a reflection of the broader generational acknowledgment that the industrial model needs to be reformed, if not entirely disposed of, for the planet to survive in the years to come.

Hipsters, in this sense, offer a radically nostalgic but progressive way to the future, and a practical recipe to build a new "good life" ideal. Hipsters look back to practices and cultures of the pre-industrial era as a means to repurpose the relationship between work and consumption in society, rethink established conceptions of social status and envisage a more sustainable societal model – created by, and catering for, the needs, values and aspirations of the Millennials generation. As a model, it is not fully formed; it is incoherent, contradictory and perhaps destined to fall apart in the long run. But still: we should probably look at hipster cultures and practices not just with mockery or snobbery, but as an experimentation camp for a "good life" ideal of the twenty-first century. If Boomers' regressive nostalgia is for an industrial society that is disappearing – but that they've actually grown in, experienced and lived – the progressive nostalgia of urban, well-educated and creative post-middle class hipsters is for a pre-industrial society they *haven't* actually lived, but that they see as more authentic than the societal model of the postwar era, and that they seek to refashion in the context of present-day global digital capitalism. It is in the combination of these two forms of nostalgia that lies the nostalgic zeitgeist of the start of the twenty-first century this book argues about. Nostalgia is the cultural zeitgeist of a Western society transitioning out of the industrial era, that in its entirety looks *back* as a way to the future. Whether hipster culture will be able to develop a full-fledged "good life" ideal remains to be seen: but if there is a progressive future ahead, some of the practices that belong to hipster culture will almost certainly have to be part of it.

Will hipsters save the world, then?

Sometimes, my friends and I have joked that "hipsters are going to save the world."

Witnessing the blossoming of hipster culture from a niche fad to a mainstream trait of twenty-first century popular culture, I slowly but consistently started to believe there is some truth in this joke.

Largely incorrectly, hipster culture has been often described as a subculture that, in the tradition of British cultural studies, is deemed to resist capitalist commercialization.[23] On the contrary, albeit it shares some stylistic traits with other subcultures, hipster culture ultimately consists in a set of practices that stem from (and do not markedly disengage from) a typically neoliberal individualistic ethos. In the famous "White Negro" essay by Norman Mailer, included in the collection entitled *Advertisements for Myself* (1957) and considered a seminal analysis on hipsters, Mailer defines the hipster as an "American existentialist," a "philosophical psychopath" who lives in a continuous present, engaging in desire and sublimation, in a constant tension between rebellion and the cult of oneself, struggling to find a seat at the table in the emergent consumer capitalist era.[24] The hipsters of the start of the twenty-first century are connoted by a similar attitude. The capacity by hipsters to discern between an ordinary taste and a marginal taste as a status-seeking practice is a feature of the hipster as the archetypal "subject in transition" from one societal phase to another. As argued by Tiziano Bonini, ultimately the end goal of a hipster is to be somebody else – hence, the commonsensical perception of the hipster as a "wannabe."[25] While this often entails class or inter-generational conflict, late-modern hipsters want to be somebody else irrespective of existing social hierarchies: in this sense they are the perfect byproduct of neoliberalism as a gentrifier of class relations. However up or down in the existing social structure, hipsters represent the manifestation of the attempt to detach from the failure of the twentieth century "good life" ideal and the strive to create a new one, whose values are found in the nostalgic recuperation of a pre-industrial authenticity.

Consumer culture scholar Janna Michael notes that hipsters embody a tension between trendiness on the one hand, and individuality and authenticity on the other. This, Michael highlights, is articulated in a rejection of the modernist notion of "breaking with the past" in favor of innovation and experimentation. The same, almost obsessive use of the term "craft" and the constant reference to an artisanal, "authentic" imaginary ultimately testifies how hipsters put in practice the romantic revival of "a sincere and pre-industrial past" as the source for authenticity, and not just in the food sector.[26] A proliferation of small-scale, nostalgic entrepreneurial endeavors can in fact be witnessed also in fashion, jewelry or product design, whereby independent producers sell handmade or artisanal objects whose market value is comparatively higher precisely because of their non-industrial production process.

These deploy a tension to "making" that is akin to the nostalgic claim of the arts and craft movement of late 1800s Britain, which promoted a return to craft practices as the source of authenticity in opposition to large-scale commodification.[27] Yet, while much of the attention to craft entails the preservation of cultural heritage, hipsters are not merely concerned with a restoration of old practices, but rather to their recuperation as a progressive endeavor, and to their adaptation to the global economy.

This is now part of a larger trend, as the "craft" label has transcended the boundaries of hipsterism to become a mainstream, global consumer trend. Hipster food chains such as BrewDog or Honest Burgers in the UK expanded from small-scale to franchise companies with a presence across different cities. Similarly, supermarkets such as Whole Foods Market sell a variety of seemingly-hipster industrial food produces, often accompanied by labels such as "organic," "natural" or "free from," that are used to mark up the authenticity of a product. These options in particular are attractive for consumers irrespective of their knowledge of the specific meaning they carry, or of the actual necessity to stick to specific dietary requirements – but because of their perceived authenticity[28] and a somewhat ethical awareness or solace. It is no coincidence that these products have acquired popularity today as hipster culture has made the quest for authenticity a matter of coolness, that the industry has turned into a marketing device. Again, the same happens also in other sectors beyond food, as large companies – take fashion giant Urban Outfitters as an example – sell items and brand themselves in accordance with the quest for authenticity and the nostalgic discourse that characterizes hipster culture. Elizabeth Currid-Halkett suggests this represents a larger tension, as a new kind of aspirational "conspicuous production":

Conspicuous production goods are a key type of aspirational class consumption. For the aspirational class, we are what we eat, drink and consume more generally, and this is why for some goods the opaque process of production has been replaced by transparency for every step. This transparency doesn't simply add value – it is the value – of many cultural goods. We will eat the smaller, sadder apples from the farmers' market because we met the farmer and we know he didn't put any nasty chemicals on his fruit...The production, rather than the consumption, becomes the key conspicuous status signal embraced by this new formation of the economic and cultural system, which is why we see the unemployed hipsters at the same coffee shop as the successful Hollywood screenwriter. Finally, after centuries of diametrical opposition, these have banded together as the aspirational class, and they want and value the same thing.[29]

In other words, while they may not *literally* save the world, it may be argued that hipsters show a possible way beyond capitalism that does *not* actually get rid of capitalism altogether – and may instead offer an entry for a remorphing of capitalism into something new. Sociologist Adam Arvidsson, for instance, argues that the reprise of old, small-scale and more sustainable practices of production and consumption such as those promoted by hipster culture should be seen as part of a wider set of phenomena pointing to the rise of a new kind of "industrious modernity." With this concept, Arvidsson seeks to grasp the frenzy around technologically-driven startup and local production cultures and their institutionalization in the global economy, in the West but also in Africa and Asia, as a mode of production constituted by labor-intensive and low-productive scenes, that draws on the "commons" that industrial capitalism has created, in order to go beyond it. The emergence of such an industrious modernity, Arvidsson argues, is set to establish as an increasingly attractive alternative to the decaying model of industrial capitalism in the years to come.[30] The question then

or2

becomes, again, what role work will occupy in the society that results out of this transition. In the next chapter, I will argue that we are converging toward a "post-employment" society.

Notes

[1] Bjorn Schiermer, "Late-modern hipsters: new tendencies in popular culture." *Acta Sociologica*, 2014, 57(2), pp. 167-81.

[2] See *ibid.*, and Janna Michael, "It's really not hip to be a hipster: negotiating trends and authenticity in the cultural field." *Journal of Consumer Culture*, 2015, 15(2), pp. 163-82.

[3] Mark Grief, "The hipster in the mirror," *New York Times*, 2010. Available at: http://pages.vassar.edu/fren380/files/2013/03/The-Sociology-of-the-Hipster-Essay-NYTimes.pdf (Last accessed 24 July 2019); Mark Grief, "What was the hipster?" *New York Magazine*, 2010. Available at: http://nymag.com/news/features/69129/ (Last accessed 24 July 2019). Similar to Grief's point, see James Cronin, Mary B. McCarthy, and Alan M. Collins. "Covert distinction: how hipsters practice food-based resistance strategies in the production of identity." *Consumption Markets & Culture*, 2014, 17, pp. 2-28.

[4] Sam Friedman, Mike Savage, Laurie Hanquinet, and Andrew Miles, "Cultural sociology and new forms of distinction." *Poetics*, 2015, 53, pp. 1-8.

[5] Andre F. Maciel, Melanie Wallendorf, "Taste engineering: an extended consumer model of cultural competence constitution." *Journal of Consumer Research* 2016, 43-5, pp. 726-46. (cf. p. 729 and p. 742).

[6] Giana Eckhardt and Fleura Bardhi, "New dynamics of social status and distinction," *Marketing Theory*, 2019, DOI: 1470593119856650.

[7] See: Sharon Zukin, "Consuming authenticity: from outposts of difference to means of exclusion." *Cultural Studies*, 2008, 22(5), pp. 724-48; Sarah Kendzior, *The view from flyover country: dispatches from the forgotten America*. New York:

Flatiron Books, 2018, pp.14-20. David Wachsmuth and Alexander Weisler, "Airbnb and the rent gap: gentrification through the sharing economy." *Environment and Planning A: Economy and Space*, 2018, 50(6), pp. 1147-70.

[8]   Richard E. Ocejo, *Masters of craft: old jobs in the new urban economy*. Princeton, NY: Princeton University Press, 2017.

[9]   Chris Land, "Back to the future: reimagining work through craft," *Futures of Work*, 2018. Available at: https://futuresofwork.co.uk/2018/11/19/back-to-the-future-re-imagining-work-through-craft/ (Last accessed 24 July 2019).

[10] "Millennial life. How young adulthood today compares with prior generations," *Pew Research Center*, 2019 Available at: https://www.pewsocialtrends.org/essay/millennial-life-how-young-adulthood-today-compares-with-prior-generations/ (Last accessed 24 July 2019).

[11] "Religion among the Millennials," *Pew Research Center*, 2010. Available at: https://www.pewforum.org/2010/02/17/religion-among-the-millennials/ (Last accessed 24 July 2019).

[12] Edoardo Schinco, "Amara Terra Mia – L'emigrazione italiana," *Senso Comune*, 2017. Available at: https://www.senso-comune.it/rivista/penisola/amara-terra-mia-lemigrazione-italiana/ (Last accessed 24 July 2019).

[13] Joel Stein, "Millennials: The Me Me Me Generation," *Time*, 2013. Available at: https://time.com/247/millennials-the-me-me-me-generation/ (Last accessed 24 July 2019).

[14] James Cairns, *The myth of the age of entitlement: Millennials, austerity, and hope*. Toronto: University of Toronto Press, 2017.

[15] See "Unemployment statistics," Eurostat, 2019. Available at: https://ec.europa.eu/eurostat/statistics-explained/index.php/Unemployment_statistics#Longer-term_unemployment_trends (Last accessed 24 July 2019).

[16] Sarah Kendzior, *The view from flyover country: dispatches*

from the forgotten America. New York: Flatiron Books, 2018.

[17] "Under pressure: the squeezed middle class," *OECD,* 2019. Available at: http://www.oecd.org/unitedstates/Middle-class-2019-United-States.pdf (Last accessed 24 July 2019).

[18] "Millennial life. How young adulthood today compares with prior generations," *Pew Research Center,* 2019 Available at: https://www.pewsocialtrends.org/essay/millennial-life-how-young-adulthood-today-compares-with-prior-generations/ (Last accessed 24 July 2019).

[19] "How Millennials voted this election," Brookings, 2016. Available at: https://www.brookings.edu/blog/fixgov/2016/11/21/how-millennials-voted/ (Last accessed 24 July 2019).

[20] "SWG-Analisi dei flussi di voto," Huffington Post Italia, 2019. Available at: https://www.huffingtonpost.it/entry/la-lega-prosciuga-di-maio_it_5cec045de4b00356fc25b556?1az=&utm_hp_ref=it-homepage#gallery/5cec092fe4b0512156f5d298/14 (Last accessed 24 July 2019).

[21] "The truth about young people and Brexit," BBC, 2018. Available at: https://www.bbc.co.uk/bbcthree/article/b8d097b0-3ad4-4dd9-aa25-af6374292de0 (Last accessed 24 July 2019).

[22] "Millennials approach baby boomers as America's largest generation in the electorate," Pew Research Center, 2018. Available at: https://www.pewresearch.org/fact-tank/2018/04/03/millennials-approach-baby-boomers-as-largest-generation-in-u-s-electorate/ (Last accessed 24 July 2019).

[23] James Cronin, Mary B. McCarthy, and Alan M. Collins. "Covert distinction: how hipsters practice food-based resistance strategies in the production of identity." *Consumption Markets & Culture,* 2014, 17, pp. 2-28.

[24] Norman Mailer, *Advertisements for myself.* Cambridge, Mass: Harvard University Press, 1959.

[25] Tiziano Bonini, *Hipster*. Milano: Doppiozero, 2014.

[26] Janna Michael, "It's really not hip to be a hipster: negotiating trends and authenticity in the cultural field." *Journal of Consumer Culture*, 2015, 15(2), pp. 163-82.

[27] See: David Gauntlett, *Making is connecting*. London: Wiley & Sons, 2013; Richard Sennett, *The Craftsman*. New Haven: Yale University Press, 2008.

[28] Sharon Zukin, "Consuming authenticity: from outposts of difference to means of exclusion." *Cultural studies*, 2008, 22(5), pp. 724-48.

[29] Elizabeth Currid-Halkett, *The sum of small things: a theory of the aspirational class*. Princeton: Princeton University Press, 2017, pp. 116-117.

[30] Adam Arvidsson, *Changemakers: the Industrious Future of the Digital Economy*. London: Polity, 2019.

4. A "post-employment" society?

This is the next century
Where the universal's free
You can find it anywhere
Yes, the future's been sold
Blur, The Universal

The next time you meet someone for the first time, try this.

Count how many exchanges before one of the two gets to ask: "What do you do?", meaning: "What is your job?" I'd suspect this will come no later than the third or fourth sentence.

There's a simple reason to it. Work largely defines and shapes the identity of a majority of people. What one does for a living is often considered equivalent to who one *is*. Societal relations, before and particularly after the affirmation of industrial modernity, have been constructed around work. The positioning of actors and social groups in society historically mirrors relations of production: in feudalism, the lords and the vassals; in industrial capitalism, the capitalists and the laborers. A lot of what we as a society are able and unable to do depends on work – our work as much as the work of others. Progressive achievements such as the welfare state, healthcare, retirement benefits, depend financially and materially upon the existence of a society constructed around work. The evolution of work, in other words, reflects and projects the evolution of society.

The inextricable overlap between one's work and one's identity that affirmed with modernity, and particularly in the second half of the twentieth century, entails that the voluntary abstinence from work – not for a day or a week, for a vacation or a break, but indefinitely – is largely regarded as an inconceivable scenario. If one does not work, it is either because one doesn't have a job – but would want to have one – or is unfit to work –

meaning, ill. As a society, it has become unthinkable to imagine people who, being able to, *do not want* to work.

As we walk through the center of her hometown on a cold December night, Clarissa tells me about her recent move from Italy to France to follow her partner, an academic, in his new job. After working in market research for years, she decided it was time to take some time back to herself. Some unspecified time. She purposely refuses to call this a sabbatical, as the term implies a state of normality – the working life – to return to at some point. She wanted instead to try out a new normality, made of not working, without a clear timeframe – and see how it goes.

What she sought to recuperate by doing so, she says, is her own sense of identity, to be found away from the definition of herself given by her work and from the regimes of productivity dictated by living a capitalist working life. She wanted to enjoy new routines and places, for these not to be the routines and places of her new job. As she makes new friends, she tells me, sometimes conversations become a bit awkward, precisely for this reason. "How come you don't want to get a job?", some ask her. "Are you ok?", some even dare question, alluding to some unspeakable illness that prevents her from working. *Work, work, work*. Sometimes people even struggle as to what to converse about with her, she says, because she does not work.

While she tells me these stories she shrugs, implying she expected such reactions. She understands she is in a privileged position, since many would not be able to economically afford to take an indefinite break from earning a salary. She underlines that, as a feminist, she is not at ease with the arrangements her current situation entails, as she is factually living on her partner's salary. She clearly states she does not want this state of things to last forever. Still, she talks about her decision as some kind of political stance – an experiment, she says, to abstain from the work-centered demands of modern living. As we move on to another topic in our conversation, I find myself somewhat jealous of her freedom.

Yet, Clarissa is very much an exception in a society otherwise obsessed with work, where swathes of people cannot afford to put themselves in question, economically and personally, as Clarissa does. Instead, most people desperately look for *any* kind of job, often unsuccessfully, upon which to build their lives, or simply pay their bills. Many work in unsatisfactory jobs, sometimes more than one job at the same time, weekdays and weekends, only to make ends meet. At the same time, however, the social pact based on the abundance of jobs and the utopia of full employment that established in the second half of the twentieth century is crumbling in front of our very eyes. Nostalgia, as seen, is the spirit that animates the response to this state of things by different groups in society. Yet, if we are in fact transitioning to a society whereby work is no longer the structure of certainty and the baseline for living a "good life," what will said society look like? Particularly, what does work look like, in this kind of society? I am not one for predictions, but based on where we are now, I would argue we are converging toward a "post-employment" society.

The future of work and the present of work: enter the "post-employment" society

Arguably, work practices and cultures have changed significantly since the postwar era, particularly in the short span of the early twenty-first century. The combination of decades of neoliberal policies with a devastating economic crisis (of which deregulated neoliberalism is also a cause) and the long-term consequences of globalization, as variously described in the book, are nonetheless only part of a more complex story that has also a lot to do with technological advancement.

Without being technologically deterministic, yet arguably work and technological advancement historically go hand-in-hand – and society changes with them. Like machines at the dawn of the industrial era, in the new century digital technologies have been a disruptive force in the domain of work, facilitating the diffusion of new and controversial practices and, in particular, enabling the blurring of the boundary between work and leisure time typical of the modern era. This brought forward the perception of a new "great transformation" in society, à la Polanyi, resulting also from the arrival of technologies such as big data, platforms, algorithms, robotics and other forms of artificial intelligence. This whole set of changes has ignited a fresh revival of the decades-old debate about "the future of work."

The question of "the future of work" has enjoyed significant popularity at regular intervals in history, usually in coincidence with the appearance of some kind of technological innovation that threatens to suppress human labor. First were, famously, the Luddites, who rose to prominence in nineteenth-century Britain as they sought to destroy textile machinery that they considered a threat to their craft, and have since then become the epitome of opposition to any kind of technological innovation.[1] After the Luddites, the fear of machines and their job-stealing potential has regularly resurfaced at almost every decade of the twentieth century, from the 1920s all the way to the 1990s.[2] For one, see this excerpt from a 1961 article of *TIME Magazine*, reported in an article by economist David Autor for the *Journal of Economics Perspective,* that discusses technological innovation of machinery in factory work:

> the number of jobs lost to more efficient machines is only part of the problem. What worries many job experts more is that automation may prevent the economy from creating enough new jobs. Throughout industry, the trend has been to bigger production with a smaller work force. Many of the losses in factory jobs have been countered by an increase

in the service industries or in office jobs. But automation is beginning to move in and eliminate office jobs too. In the past, new industries hired far more people than those they put out of business. But this is not true of many of today's new industries. Today's new industries have comparatively few jobs for the unskilled or semiskilled, just the class of workers whose jobs are being eliminated by automation.[3]

Jump 20 years later, to the 1980s, and you will find a new iteration of the same concerns. The arrival of computers in offices was seen as a deadly threat for human labor. Computers were deemed to be able to rationalize the recourse to human resources and henceforth lead to a reduction of employed office staff.[4] Inevitably, analogous preoccupations have resurfaced today that digital technologies of all sorts have made their way into the workplace and in society at large.

Warnings about the disappearance of jobs are heard almost daily, usually related to the looming arrival of robots and the threat of large-scale job automation. This brings a mixture of excitement and concern: Eric Bjornolfsson and Andrew McAfee, for instance, have argued that we are experiencing a revolution driven by technological advancements, that will fundamentally redefine work and the economy at large. They call this a "second machine age," the first being the Industrial Revolution, and predict the large-scale automation of a variety of menial and cognitive tasks, accompanied by a further rise in social inequality as a result of this systemic shift.[5]

Similarly, a myriad of reports has appeared in recent years, that analyze trends and make predictions about the "future of work." These usually offer first-hand data about the present condition of the labor market (which are, indeed, very useful) together with more or less wild speculations about what is going to happen. Perhaps the most famous among them is the "Technology at Work" report by Oxford scholars Carl Benedikt

Frey and Martin Osborne, which estimates that almost half of currently-existing jobs are at risk of being automated in the coming decades. Frey and Osborne write that:

> While computerization has been historically confined to routine tasks involving explicit rule-based activities... algorithms for big data are now rapidly entering domains reliant upon pattern recognition and can readily substitute for labour in a wide range of non-routine cognitive tasks. In addition, advanced robots are gaining enhanced senses and dexterity, allowing them to perform a broader scope of manual tasks...This is likely to change the nature of work across industries and occupations.[6]

Many other reports produced similar predictions, albeit sometimes envisaging less alarming scenarios. Using data from the US Bureau of Statistics, a 2017 research by consultancy company McKinsey for instance predicts that, while automation will impact industries widely, ultimately "technology creates more jobs than it destroys." Nonetheless, the report also warns that "employment shifts can be painful."[7] *Oh, really? Who could have guessed?*

In a similar vein, a 2019 OECD report photographs the transformation of a labor market shifting away from manufacturing (20 percent of jobs lost in this sector between 1995 and 2015) and toward the service economy (where jobs grew by 27 percent in the same timeframe). Discussing this evolution, the report cautiously predicts that only 14 percent of jobs are at risk of being automated in the coming decades, but also underlines that another 32 percent could "change drastically." In the end, however, it takes an optimistic view: "Will this lead to fewer jobs for humans?" the report asks. "Unlikely", it answers, arguing that: "While technological progress makes some occupations obsolete, it also creates new jobs."[8]

Robots aside, the rapid diffusion of big data, algorithms and artificial intelligence, together with radical technological innovation in factory work – labeled as Industry 4.0 or a "fourth industrial revolution" – exacerbated the perception of a dramatic, technologically-driven shift, potentially leading to a massive disappearance of jobs. Yet, as both writer Kevin Baker and sociologist Paul Thompson highlight, predictions of doom about the future of work that have appeared in previous decades have historically proven to be exaggerated: "(I)f we look at the existing and projected patterns of polarized job growth and what we know about their labor processes – caring, interactive service roles, emotional labour, professional, creative and high tech, it is much harder to see extensive displacement through robotization or AI," Thompson argues. "(I)t is tasks, not whole occupations that will disappear or be reconfigured."[9] And yet: there is a common perception that this time is different. Why?

I would argue that a rather static view has connoted the cultural conception of work in society since the postwar era and up to the present day. If we think about it, the codification of labor time into legally-binding employment contracts, stipulated with mutual consent between one party and another, is actually an invention of industrialization. Prior to that, feudal work did not entail employment as a market exchange; it was customary codes, tradition and honor that regulated the relationship between a lord and a vassal. It is capitalism, and particularly industrial modernity, that developed employment relations as codified forms of engagement to impose bureaucratic control upon workers.[10] What's more, employment relations codified into law as a reflection of the duality of the relations of production of the industrial era, which juxtaposed – to use Marxist jargon – those who own the means of production vis-à-vis those who sell their labor-power for money, and entangled them into a market exchange. These arrangements are, in other words, quite peculiar to when they were created, and reflect the larger, conflicting relations they were meant to mediate. Yet, the very same categories, and the fixed cultural conception of work these embody, are still what we use to interpret work today, their adequacy largely taken for granted in the public discourse about work. The cultural conception of work in society today is still the cultural conception of work we inherited from the industrial and postwar era, which determines that work has a clearly-defined temporality – commonly represented by the 9-to-5 trope – and spatiality, as one must go to a designated location – the workplace – to execute tasks that are coordinated when not ordered, supervised when not surveilled, by another human being.

However, work in the twenty-first century exudes established conventions of leisure and labor time, temporality and spatiality of execution. What if, actually, the question about the future of work is not one of job automation and robots replacing humans, but rather a question about whether the codes and structures by which we define employment are rendered obsolete? What if, in the demise of the industrial order, we are transitioning to a society in which work is deprived of its fixed normative dimension, of the structured temporality and spatiality prescribed by the employment contract, in favor of a fluid – liquid, Zygmunt Bauman would say[11] – context made of activities that can be undoubtedly classified as work, but actually take place away from the twentieth century definition of employment?

* * *

Welcome to the "post-employment" society.

* * *

The term "post-employment" aims to account for the proliferation of forms of work that deviate from the normatively-codified, culturally established definitions of work typical of the industrial era, which are reflected in the "standard" employment contract. I take this term, "post-employment," from Sarah Kendzior, who uses it to describe the extremely precarious conditions that a variety of middle- and working-class Americans experience in the aftermath of the 2007-8 economic crisis.[12] However, I conceive of the notion of "post-employment" beyond precarious work. On the contrary, with this term I seek to describe a wide range of old and new jobs, mostly but not exclusively undertaken on a digital platform or enabled by one, characterized by practices of codification of the labor process that partly diverge from those of the industrial era, and that therefore cannot be adequately reconciled under existing understandings. Freelancers, "click workers," "on-demand" laborers of any sort, but also "digital nomads" and startuppers: all these are, broadly and loosely intended, subjects who engage in forms of work that escape the classifications and the normative boundaries created in the industrial era. Instead, they represent the most conspicuous manifestation of the ongoing transition from a static conception of work, typical of the industrial model, to a set of practices which cannot be properly understood, culturally and societally, by using those categories.

Inside "post-employment" work: the gig economy

Albeit not exclusively, the diffusion of digital technologies, big data and algorithms in work is indeed a key component in the shift toward a "post-employment" society. The landmark feature of "post-employment" work is, in fact, the invisibilization of relations of production which takes place as a result of the "platformization" of the meeting between supply and demand of work, enabled by digital technologies. The phenomenon known as the "gig economy" is where this can be observed more closely.

The gig economy represents a "post-employment" model of work organization by which a digital platform intermediates the commission of a task, that is demanded by a consumer or client and executed by a paid worker. Gig economy platforms therefore act at the same time as market intermediaries and pseudo-employers of on-demand workers, who are legally classified by these companies as self-employed. For their intermediation role, platforms charge a percentage fee on the basis of the value of the "gig." The gig economy encompasses a variety of different kinds of work, ranging from creative freelancing to menial, alienating digital-based micro tasks – also known as "click-work" – and is peculiarly identified with consumer-based services of urban ride-hailing and delivery of goods, epitomised by apps such as Uber and Deliveroo.[13]

Over the years, these apps have become quite popular especially in global cities around the world, particularly in sectors such as transportation and hospitality, where they can offer a cheaper alternative to public and other private services. Their success, however, has run in parallel with criticism against the self-employed status of these workers, that does not match the reality of these jobs and how workers are managed. Also, the working conditions to which these apps subject their workers, who are available "on tap"[14] to fulfill existing demand at a given time, have been under scrutiny. Research has accounted that gig workers are usually poorly paid and have to work long hours in order to earn a decent salary. These among other aspects also ignited forms of mobilization by workers worldwide, who campaigned for minimum wage, sick pay and other welfare provisions.[15]

Most interestingly, gig workers are on the front line of a model of organization of work whereby, to put it in the words of *Financial Times* journalist Sarah O'Connor, "the boss is an algorithm."[16] The "Uber Game," also developed by the *Financial Times* in 2017 and based on interviews with Uber drivers, provides an interesting snippet of a day in the life of a gig worker. Faced with the simulation of working for Uber for a week, the player-driver is prompted with a number of decisions to take, and gradually confronted with a number of issues. At the end of the week, a report is given of how one has scored compared to a real-life Uber driver. Invariably, the game shows that drivers earn very poorly, work long hours and their continuity of work is constantly on the line, being dependent upon the reputational scores they are able to achieve and maintain as a result of the reviews given by customers after each ride.[17] Did you watch the opening episode of Season Three of Black Mirror, *Nosedive,* which portrays a world in which everyone rates each other, and everything goes very wrong because of how ratings determine people's lives and conceptions of worth? Well, basically that's what working in the gig economy looks like.

Sometimes, however, the invisible managerial relations that characterize these forms of work actually become visible, thanks to glitches in the algorithmic workings of these platforms. During the London Bridge terror attack of June 2017, for instance, many of the victims used Uber to escape from the scene. Unable to recognize what was going on, the Uber algorithm that regulates the value of each ride, which dynamically aligns with demand, automatically triggered a price surge as a result of the high number of incoming requests. Users quickly turned to social media to voice their disgust, causing the company to ultimately refund those affected.[18] In a less dramatic, but no less disturbing example, during a heavy snowstorm that hit London in the early days of March 2018 – which caused the Met Office to issue a warning to stay indoors and avoid traveling around the city unless strictly necessary – Deliveroo offered its workers a "fee boost" of £1 per delivery, communicated to workers in the form of relentless phone notifications, as an incentive to work more intensely in arguably very dangerous conditions.

* * *

Deliveroo "fee boost," London, March 2018. Source: https://
twitter.com/Rstlau7/status/969637271107403782 (Last accessed
24 April 2019)

* * *

As soon as couriers posted screenshots like the above on social media, the Deliveroo "fee boost" gathered a lot of media attention, to the point that, in the attempt to mitigate a potential public relations crisis, a spokesperson for Deliveroo told the press that "a £1 surge is automatically applied whenever the number of their orders increases by a significant amount, with a £2 per order surge provided for their riders." In other words: *it's the algorithm, stupid!*[19]

As a paradigmatic example of the "post-employment" evolution of work here discussed, the gig economy demonstrates that the "standard" or "nonstandard" contractual status of a worker is an important but no longer primary or determinant aspect to consider when looking at work today, its quality and conditions, its understanding and meaning. Also, focusing primarily on the contractual status of a worker incidentally induces one to take a quite nostalgic positioning, which implicitly assumes not only that industrial work conditions were better – which may be, on pure terms, somewhat true – but also a viable scenario to return to. Yet, this clashes not only with technological advancement but also with the fact that many gig workers do not actually aspire to "go back" and be employees. The claim of independence at the heart of the gig economy is in fact among the main elements of attractiveness for workers toward it. This kind of work offers them a sense of self-determination that is largely preferable to being in a "bullshit job" like those described by David Graeber in his vitriolic account of neoliberal work.[20] See for instance how this Deliveroo courier describes his employer:

> We don't hate Deliveroo – we may resent them for how they've treated us, but overall, we want them to succeed – it benefits us as much as it does them. We'd like to form a good relationship with our employer, to the benefit of wages and profits across the board.[21]

Furthermore, and perhaps most importantly, the gig economy

implicitly, and sometimes also explicitly, represents a prospective model for the organization and platformization of *all* work – particularly, but not solely, unskilled and low-skilled work. This, after all, is not new, as testified by Daniel Pink's "free agent nation" vision.[22] Digital technology, however, makes possible to cater for forms of work that are not temporally or spatially arranged according to the industrial model, enabling work to become a constellation of tasks the execution of which is regulated, coordinated and surveilled by a combination of big data and algorithms. When a worker's boss is an algorithm, to paraphrase Sarah O'Connor, one takes orders from one's phone – which, as a data machine, becomes also a powerful instrument of control, as it constantly and granularly monitors a worker's productivity and usefulness. Gig work matters, in other words, because as a model of work organization it is an ostensible sign of the transition taking place from the industrial era towards *something else*, setting a score for what is next to come.

Which may, in fact, eventually be job automation and human replacement: if we think about it, much of the gig economy, such as ride-hailing and delivery work, could actually be substituted by a machine. Uber and Amazon, for instance, are reported to be trialing out driverless cars and drones to undertake these tasks. However, some argue this should not be a scenario to fear. They, in fact, believe the solution is actually to *demand full automation*, and build a society *without work*.

After work?

In parallel with the revival of the "future of work" debate, a current in the post-Marxist Autonomist left has brought forward the utopian idea of imagining a society constructed *without* work. The utopia of a *post-work* society is the landmark proposition in the #Accelerate Manifesto, written by critical theorists Alex Williams and Nick Srnicek in 2013, which represents the foundational text in contemporary fashionable Accelerationist

Theory. The Accelerationist approach sustains that the historical processes underpinning the evolution of capitalism should in fact be intensified – hence, "accelerated" – in order to speed up its self-destructive potential, and finally bring radical change. In Williams and Srnicek's words, there is a necessity to push "towards a future that is more modern, an alternative modernity that neoliberalism is inherently unable to generate."[23]

At the core of this push lies the idea of striving toward "full automation." In their subsequent book, the cult-like *Inventing the Future*, Williams and Srnicek argue in favor of a "fully automated economy" that does not aspire to full employment but rather uses technological advancement "to liberate humanity from the drudgery of work while simultaneously producing increasing amounts of wealth." This is, they sustain, the political proposition the left should embrace in order to develop new "postcapitalist futures." This vision is accompanied by the call for a universal basic income, that would originate from the increased wealth produced by the labor of machines and would also supplement the large-scale unemployment inevitably deriving from full automation.[24] The post-work imaginary is taken even further to the left by another critical theorist, Aaron Bastani, who argues about Fully Automated Luxury Communism, a vision whereby technology eliminates the necessity of human labor, thus making room for the advent of a communistic society in which the value of commodities is ultimately reduced to zero.[25]

Many have criticized the post-work imaginary, sometimes quite strongly. Labor scholar Paul Thompson, for instance, has noted that imaginaries of the "end of work" are by no means new, as exemplified by Jeremy Rifkin's same-titled book or Stanley Aronowitz and William DiFazio's *The Jobless Future*, incidentally both published in 1995.[26] Thompson underlines how, for many, work represents a key source of meaning, identity and sense of purpose in life irrespective of its actual quality. While he recognizes that some jobs are, indeed, pointless, Thompson opposes David Graeber's argument (echoed also in David Frayne's *Refusal of Work*)[27] that *all* work is dreary and degrading, arguing that post-work promoters overlook the satisfactory and somewhat rewarding nature of even the most low-skilled and poorly paid work – a point which, for that matter, I am largely in agreement with.[28] Furthermore, I would point out that actually Graeber inadvertently offers support to Thompson's argument: why would there be a necessity to write an emotional, powerful and compelling book about how "bullshit" work can be, if after all...*it doesn't matter*?

And yet: I would also argue that, despite the ideological or factual flaws it might have, we ought to embrace the post-work imaginary precisely as an imperfect, utopian fantasy. For how unrealistic it may be, the vision of a society without or beyond work offers in fact a positive, forward-looking and not just nostalgic fantasy to aspire to – one that we are desperately in need of. Arguably, the post-work vision struggles to appeal as widely as the nostalgic zeitgeist does; when mentioned, it is easily dismissed as unrealistic or unfeasible, particularly in relation to the companion universal basic income proposal, and is currently "hip" only among a small filter bubble of technomarxists. However, as historian Rutger Bregman notes, many ideas were long dismissed as unfeasible and unrealistic, until they became real.[29] Which brings us to the final point of this book: the rise of nostalgia is a symptom that, as a society, our capacity to imagine a future has died out. *We need to create a new imaginary.* How do we imagine a future after nostalgia?

Notes

[1]   Eric J., Hobsbawm, "The machine breakers," *Past & Present* 1, 1952, pp. 57-70.

[2]   Louis Anslow, "Robots have been about to take all the jobs for more than 200 years." *Medium*, 2016. Available at: https://timeline.com/robots-have-been-about-to-take-all-the-jobs-

for-more-than-200-years-5c9c08a2f41d (Last accessed 24 July 2019).

[3] David Autor, "Why are there still so many jobs? The history and future of workplace automation," *Journal of Economic Perspectives*, 1961, 29(3), pp. 3-30.

[4] I.R. Hoos, "When the computer takes over the office." In: D. Preece, I. McLoughlin, P. Dawson, *Technology, organisations and innovations: the early debates*, London: Routledge, 2000, 179-97.

[5] Erik Brynjolfsson and Andrew McAfee, *The second machine age: work, progress, and prosperity in a time of brilliant technologies*. New York: W.W. Norton & Company, 2014.

[6] Carl Benedikt Frey and Michael Osborne, *Technology at work. The Future of Innovation and Employment. Citi GPS: Global Perspectives & Solutionsm*, 2015, p. 208.

[7] "Five lessons from history on AI, automation, and employment," *McKinsey*, 2017. Available at: https://www.mckinsey.com/featured-insights/future-of-work/five-lessons-from-history-on-ai-automation-and-employment (Last accessed 24 July 2019).

[8] "Data on the future of work," *OECD*, 2015. Available at: https://www.oecd.org/els/emp/future-of-work/data/ (Last accessed 24 July 2019).

[9] Kevin Baker, "The future of work, a history," POLITICO, 2018. Available at: https://www.politico.com/magazine/story/2018/01/07/the-future-of-work-a-history-216244 (Last accessed 24 July 2019); Paul Thompson, 'The Refusal of Work: Past, Present and Future," *Futures of Work*, 2018. Available at: https://futuresofwork.co.uk/2018/09/05/the-refusal-of-work-past-present-and-future/ https://futuresofwork.co.uk/2018/09/05/editorial-from-the-future-of-work-to-futures-of-work/ (Last accessed 24 July 2019).

[10] Hartmut Rosa, *Social acceleration: A new theory of modernity*. New York: Columbia University Press, 2013, p. 165.

[11] Zygmunt Bauman, *Liquid modernity*, London: Wiley & Sons, 2013.

[12] Sarah Kendzior, *The view from flyover country: dispatches from the forgotten America*. Flatiron Books, 2018,

[13] Alessandro Gandini, "Labour process theory and the gig economy." *Human Relations*, 2019, 72(6), pp. 1039-56.

[14] "Workers on tap," *The Economist*, 2014. Available at: https://www.economist.com/leaders/2014/12/30/workers-on-tap (Last accessed 24 July 2019).

[15] See: Steven P. Vallas, "Platform capitalism: what's at stake for workers?" *New Labor Forum*, 2018, 28 (1), pp. 48-59.

[16] Sarah O'Connor, "When Your Boss is an Algorithm," *Financial Times*, 8 September 2016.

[17] "The Uber game," *Financial Times*, 2017. Available at: https://ig.ft.com/uber-game/

[18] "Uber has refunded customers caught up in London terror attack," *Business Insider*, 2017. Available at: https://www.businessinsider.com/uber-refunds-customers-surge-pricing-london-terror-attack-2017-6?IR=T (Last accessed 24 July 2019).

[19] UK weather: "Deliveroo faces criticism over driver safety in heavy snow," *The Independent*, 2018. Available at: https://www.independent.co.uk/life-style/food-and-drink/deliveroo-driver-safety-uk-weather-snow-criticism-extra-charge-delivery-a8236966.html (Last accessed 24 July 2019).

[20] David Graeber, *Bullshit jobs*. New York, NY: Simon & Schuster, 2018.

[21] Mark Graham, Joe Shaw, *Towards a fairer gig economy*. London: Meatspace Press, 2017, p. 9.

[22] Daniel H. Pink, *Free agent nation: how America's new independent workers are transforming the way we live*. Business Plus, 2001.

[23] Alex Williams and Nick Srnicek, *#ACCELERATE MANIFESTO for an Accelerationist Politics*, 2013. Available

at: http://criticallegalthinking.com/2013/05/14/accelerate-manifesto-for-an-accelerationist-politics/ (Last accessed 24 July 2019).

[24] Nick Srnicek and Alex Williams, *Inventing the future: postcapitalism and a world without work*. London: Verso, 2015, p. 109.

[25] Aaron Bastani, *Fully automated luxury communism*. London: Verso, 2019.

[26] Jeremy Rifkin, *The end of work*. New York: Putnam, 1995; Stanley Aronowitz and William DiFazio, *The jobless future: sci-tech and the dogma of work*. Minneapolis: University of Minnesota Press, 1994.

[27] David Frayne, *The refusal of work*. London: Zed Books, 2015.

[28] Paul Thompson, "The refusal of work: past, present and future," *Futures of Work*, 2018. Available at: https://futuresofwork.co.uk/2018/09/05/the-refusal-of-work-past-present-and-future/ https://futuresofwork.co.uk/2018/09/05/editorial-from-the-future-of-work-to-futures-of-work/ (Last accessed 24 July 2019).

[29] Rutger Bregman, *Utopia for realists: and how we can get there*. London: Bloomsbury Publishing, 2017.

5. After nostalgia

These men look the same as they have always looked
They talk as they have always talked
But before your eyes they are changing
Public Service Broadcasting, Progress

In the words of German economic sociologist Wolfgang Streeck:

> The old order that was destroyed by the onslaught of the populist barbarians in 2016 was the state system of global capitalism. What the still to be created new order will look like is uncertain, as is to be expected of an interregnum. An interregnum in Gramsci's sense is a period of tremendous insecurity in which the accustomed chains of cause and effect are no longer in force, and unexpected, dangerous and grotesquely abnormal events may occur at any moment. Disparate lines of development run unreconciled, parallel to one another, resulting in unstable configurations of many kinds, and chains of surprising events take the place of predictable structures.[1]

Nostalgia, I have argued, is the cultural zeitgeist of this interregnum.

For Lauren Berlant, the decline of the "good life" ideal has led to an "impasse," intended as "a time of dithering from which someone or some situation cannot move forward." This impasse takes place as "the traditional infrastructures for reproducing life – at work, in intimacy, politically – are crumbling at a threatening pace," to the point of creating the perception of living "a middle with no boundaries, edges, or shape." Today, she argues, the most precarious fractions of the population who used to be physically and economically protected in society are coping with the collective loss of the fantasy of the "good life."[2]

In this interregnum – we could continue, drawing from Streeck – "unexpected, dangerous and grotesquely abnormal events" take place, such as Brexit and the Trump election, in parallel with other, superficially disconnected and heterogeneous but culturally coherent and relevant phenomena, such as the surge of hipster culture. These are different manifestations of a same zeitgeist, which reflects the acknowledgment that the collective sense of purpose and shared direction to an imagined destination – the future – is lost. The past, as a result, becomes a safe harbor to take shelter in, until the storm will pass.

Both nostalgic answers to the demise of the societal model based on work as a conduit to the "good life" described in this book, however, do not represent viable societal visions for the future but, indeed, fantasies, that are difficult to project beyond their singularity.

On the one hand, the retrotopia of going back to the societal model of the postwar era is simply unrealistic. Looking at the societal evolution of the last few decades, actually one might argue that Baby Boomers are ultimately right to be nostalgic. Yet, albeit romantically appealing, the coal mine jobs promised by Trump will not actually come back, and neither will a version of the British Empire based on tea, jam and biscuit exports as former Tory leadership contender Andrea Leadsom once claimed.[3] The nostalgic promise of Brexit and Trump ignores the irreversible changes that the last decades have brought in society, culture and technology, from which it is factually impossible to come back. We might not like to live in a global economy, and that's fair. Global capitalism may be in crisis, as Streeck points out, and we might as well promote policies that countenance to some degree the distortions of "globalism," as Brexit and Trump fans call it. But to promise a return to a pre-global, predominantly white world, where immigrants "go back to their fucking country," as I was myself once told, is against the tide of history.

On the other hand, hipster progressive nostalgia is equally difficult to project beyond post-middle class urban circles. What hipster culture proposes, in fact, is a more acceptable and ethically-mindful, but nonetheless rather individualistic version of the neoliberal vision of work and society – what Carolina Bandinelli and I described as "collaborative individualism"[4] – adapted to the post-neoliberal era. The hipster alternative requires a fair amount of cultural but also social and economic capital to be sustained, that many simply are deprived of, or prevented to have access to – not to mention the different kinds of inequality and the various contradictions which inhabit hipster culture, such as the processes of ruthless gentrification and real estate speculation, the increasing relevance of corporate interests, the pervasive presence of marketing hype.

A combination of these options looks no more viable, as the values underpinning the positions of Trump/Brexit voters and hipsters on social issues are diametrically opposed if not irreconcilable. The Trump/Brexit imaginary is soaked in a masculine, patriarchal culture that opposes gender equality and sees political correctness as the "great corrupter" of what Western society traditionally used to be in the middle of the twentieth century – especially in the Trump case, an ethnically homogeneous (white), male-dominated, religious-fearing society. Hipsters, on the other hand, are not at all nostalgic on this front, as they promote a radically progressive set of ideals based on diversity and openness, support gender equality and LGBTQ rights, and oppose discrimination of racial and sexual minorities. While its aesthetics recuperate an old idea of masculinity, exemplified by big men's beards and the noble fatigue of working-class jobs, hipster culture is nonetheless infused of a gay masculinity, often advocated for by "feminist men" who are open about their intimacy and accept their weaknesses not as a sign of vulnerability, but as a display of strength.

* * *

So, where do we go from here?

* * *

A first step might be to acknowledge that, albeit the current populist fantasy of nostalgia looks quite dramatic, society has actually been through similar phases before. This is one feature of nostalgia we haven't discussed yet: among other things, in fact, nostalgia is *recursive*.

Recursive nostalgia

In the previous chapter we met the Luddites. Their machine-breaking protests in the early 1800s, during the first Industrial Revolution, were not an isolated, momentary lapse of nostalgia in an otherwise smooth timeline. Luddite riots began in 1811 and lasted until 1816-17; concomitantly, in 1814-15 the Congress of Vienna redesigned the layout of Western Europe as a response to the revolutionary ideals that emerged in the late eighteenth century, which were seen as a threat to the status quo. Roughly in the same timeframe, romanticism affirms as a set of ideals opposing the rational and moral values of Enlightenment, in favor of a primacy of emotions and authenticity. Romanticism, one might argue, was a kind of nostalgic wave, propaedeutic to a phase of societal change based on the spread of nationalistic ideals. [5]

Similarly, toward the end of the 1800s, as a typical symptom of *fin de siècle* anxiety, the Decadent movement (and its cognate variations of Symbolism and Aestheticism) might be seen as a kind of nostalgic transition prior to the rationalist and futuristic push brought by modernity, conveyed in the form of a celebration of pleasure, of the present moment and of the authentic. Epitomized in Britain by Oscar Wilde, in France by *poets maudits* Charles Baudelaire and Arthur Rimbaud and novelist Joris-Karl Huysmans, the Decadent movement must be seen in juxtaposition to the avant-garde movements, particularly Futurism, that will become hugely popular at the start of the twentieth century in their promotion of modernity as a radical break from the past. (Interestingly, Des Esseintes, the protagonist of the novel *A Rebour* by Joris-Karl Huysmans and an archetypal Decadent character, is said to be an inspirational figure for Pete Doherty, leader of the band The Libertines and icon of the indie subculture, who even wrote a song titled "A Rebours").[6]

These examples suggest that nostalgia, loosely intended, should be seen as a recursive societal trait – more precisely, a cultural marker of societal turning points. Its emergence in various peculiar forms at different stages in history represents the symptom of a repurposing of the relationship between rationality and emotion, between science and spirit, taking place in coincidence with moments of societal transformation. As an intermediary between rationality and spirit, nostalgia can take different forms: romantic nostalgia is peculiarly different from decadent nostalgia, as well as from present-day nostalgia. Sometimes, this nostalgic reaction takes the form of a liberation fight from an imagined Other – today: migrants, the EU, the economic elites – blamed for the corruption of what used to be a golden age deemed to last forever. Yet, it remains the sign of a turning point: in times of passage, nostalgia becomes a way to cope with, and sometimes to resist, what is perceived as an incoming, dramatic societal and cultural shift. Then, the past becomes an idealized place to search for a lost authenticity, as an acknowledgment that a moment of change is coming. If we think about it, the same happens also in our everyday lives. When something is about to change we look back, reminisce and think about the past.

Sociologist Hartmut Rosa argues we are experiencing a phase of acceleration of social change at the start of the twenty-first century, characterized by a "shrinking of the present" and the perception of a "frenetic standstill." Acceleration, Rosa underlines, is a constitutive part of modernity; in late modernity, however, it "crosses a critical threshold...beyond which the demand for societal synchronization and social integration can no longer be met."[7] The modernization process, Rosa shows, is characterized by "waves of acceleration" produced by "technical innovation and their industrial implementation." From the introduction of the steam engine and railroads to the diffusion of telecommunications, from the telegraph and the telephone up to the Internet: all these waves, he contends, "altered the lifeworld and everyday culture in occasionally shocking and traumatic ways and led to a shifting sense...of being-in-time and being-in-the-world," leading to a "call for deceleration and the nostalgic desire for the lost 'slow world.'"[8] Thus, the perception of a crisis, identified first by postmodern theorists in the 1980s as the fall of grand narratives and the demise of ideology, has finally materialized today into an actual crisis, characterized by what Rosa calls a "contemporization," that is the perception of an instantaneous time. "The acceleration of social relations rooted in modernity," Rosa claims, "takes on a new quality such that the linearity and sequentiality of the perception and processing of problems and changes, at both individual and social levels, is broken up and the aspiration to integration is abandoned."[9]

Discussing what comes after the present temporal disalignment, Rosa outlines four possible scenarios. One is "the formation of a new form of institutional facilitation and stabilization of the acceleration process," leading up to "a new equilibrium." This, he continues, would "repeat the organizational and orientational achievements of modernity," such as the welfare state, by replacing them with more dynamic arrangements that reconcile with the speed of late modernity." This, he claims, is an "unrealistic" option, since it is difficult to see how such reforms would be able to "withstand" the dialectical logic of acceleration, thus inevitably leading up to a "short" second modernity. A second scenario is "the definitive abandonment of the project of modernity, which could lead to the emergence of genuinely 'post-modern' forms of subjectivity and a new kind of (sub-)politics" – somewhat akin to the post-work scenario earlier discussed – the success of which, he claims, is difficult to foresee. A third one – actually the fourth in his typology, that he sees as the most likely – is the final collapse of the modern social order, an "unbridled rush into the abyss" made of nuclear or climatic catastrophes and "an eruption of uncontrolled violence." However, the third scenario he sees is that we "reach the emergency break" of acceleration, what Walter Benjamin conceived as an "exit from history" and a "revolution against progress."[10] This, I argue, actually captures the nostalgic zeitgeist of the start of the twenty-first century.

Progress

The future as a collective sense of purpose and shared direction to an imagined destination is a social and cultural construction that does not simply materialize spontaneously. On the contrary, the imaginary of a future gets to be created over time, for it to become actualized once it becomes hegemonic, and henceforth desirable, among large parts of the population. In the present interregnum, the demise of the societal model of the twentieth century postwar era, based on work as a conduit to living the "good life," is accompanied by the demise of the idea of the future as progress that developed in the same timeframe. Twenty-first century nostalgia, in other words, is also a revolution against progress.

As said, following the two wars the era of optimism that began in the West was characterized by a sense of excitement about the future and a widespread *belief* in progress. The very own idea of progress was incarnated by America. "America is the original version of modernity," writes Jean Baudrillard in his beautiful, same-name 1986 pamphlet. For Baudrillard, America is "utopia achieved"; to land in America, writes Baudrillard, is "to land in that 'religion' of the way of life that Tocqueville described... where success and action are seen as profound illustrations of the moral law." Baudrillard underlines the mythical character of the American way of life, that he considers incarnated by the shopping mall and the cars driven around vast deserted lands. Yet, like many of its postmodern contemporaries, he sees mid-1980s America in crisis – the crisis of "an achieved utopia," writes Baudrillard, "built on the idea that (America) is the realization of everything the others have dreamt of – justice, plenty, rule of law, wealth, freedom: it knows this, it believes in it, and in the end, the others have come to believe in it too." The crisis Baudrillard described presciently, and that we now see in full today, is the crisis in the belief of American capitalism as the conveyor of progress. "The fifties," Baudrillard concludes, "were the real high spot for the US ('when things were going on')." Already in 1986, he notes a rising nostalgia for the postwar era, "for the ecstasy of power, when power held power. In the Seventies power was still there, but the spell was broken. That was orgy time (war, sex, Manson, Woodstock). Today the orgy is over."[11]

A testimony to the postwar times as an era of optimism and American power is Walt Disney's "Carousel of Progress," a theater attraction created by General Electric and commissioned to Disney for 1964's New York's World Fair, then moved to Disneyland's Tomorrowland where it remained open between 1967 and 1973. The Carousel of Progress celebrated the ideal of the "good life" as described in this book, and particularly the role of technology in making life easier for families. Bob Sullivan recounts the rise – and fall – of this illusion:

On stage 1, theater-goers met an extended family in their home at the dawn of the 20th century, (unknowingly) struggling with a hand-cranked washing machine, a gas lamp, and other primitive household technologies of the day. In stage 2, during the 1920s, life had improved a bit, with electric lighting, a sewing machine, and a radio making an appearance. When stage 3 rolled around, in the 1940s, a television and a washing machine have made life considerably easier. But the final stage offered a glimpse of digital utopia. "I'm thrilled with my new dishwasher," proclaims Sarah, the mother of the family. Freed of yet another household chore by automation, she now has more time to join "garden club, a literary society, a ladies bowling league." Husband John enjoys a similar boon of free time, thanks to modernity. All the while, the animatrons urge members of the audience to join them as they break into song, belting out the ride's theme, "It's a Great, Big Beautiful Tomorrow" – the melody sounds a bit like It's a Small World. Millions left the ride humming the catchy tune, convinced that innovation and ambitious corporations were going to fill our lives with leisure time and pleasure. Where did it all go so wrong?[12]

It went wrong, Sullivan concludes, as the relationship between work, leisure and technology became toxic, with work eating up leisure time and paving the way for the always-on lives of the neoliberal era. As Zygmunt Bauman notes, "The first thing to leap to mind whenever 'progress' is mentioned is, for many of us, the prospect of more jobs for humans – those requiring intellectual skills as much as the already-vanished manual ones – that are bound to soon disappear, replaced by computers and computer-managed robots."[13] The demise of a society based on work ultimately put not just the "good life" ideal, but the imaginary of *any* future, into an irredeemable crisis. As seen, a key component in the ideal of progress is that technology, in particular, is there to ameliorate people's lives, leading to future prosperity. As a creative product, science fiction significantly contributed to tying the belief in technology and the future with the belief in American capitalism. Decades of science fiction presented the public with scenarios of technological utopias and dystopias of all sorts. Flying cars, androids, teleportation: science fiction futures caused a glow of fascination in the minds of many, as an exciting, somewhat frightening but overall desirable prospect, characterized by one certainty: if something went wrong, Americans would come to the rescue. The belief in the future that science fiction, even in its dystopian tales, was pervaded by, largely went betrayed. As Daniel H. Wilson underlines: 'The future is now and we're not impressed… The time has come to hold the golden age of science fiction accountable for its fantastic promises."[14]

Perhaps the most iconic representation of progress as the social and cultural construction of the future in the twentieth century – and yet a glamorous manifestation of its current demise – is the race for space. Millions of people all over the world tuned in to their televisions to witness the moon landing on 20 July 1969, when Neil Armstrong put human feet on the lunar ground for the first time. A sense of collective achievement pervaded Western society following the moon landing, which reinforced people's belief in the American way to the future and in capitalism as the recipe to achieve the betterment of society. Today, 50 years later, the moon landing is the protagonist of one of the most famous conspiracy theories across the Internet, which alleges it has actually never taken place, but was instead an American publicity stunt designed to project an imaginary of power and strength against the USSR at the peak of the Cold War. While conspiracy theories about the moon landing have existed since the day after the event, they have found new life in the online era, to the point that between 5 percent and 20 percent of Americans today reportedly doubt it has ever happened.[15]

This shows how the crisis of progress is also, more broadly, a crisis of the societal trust in science as a propeller of life improvement. This is connoted by nostalgia for when progress did not pay so much attention to the consequences of the impact of human action on the planet. Trump, again, leads the pack here, as he repeatedly denied the existence of climate change and ultimately pulled the US out of the Paris Climate Agreement. But it's not just Trump: a distrust for science and expertise runs deep at the microsocial level of individual citizens, demonstrated for one by the anti-vaccine crusade, that alleges some vaccines are conveyors of autism – in spite of scientific proof of the contrary. As many have argued, we have entered a *post-truth* era[16;] the damage this large-scale distrust in science will do in the long term remains to be seen.

In the meantime, we can see how the nostalgic revolution against progress is a symmetrical reflection of the fact that we are unable to conceive of the future. As noted by Simon Reynolds, "today we seem to have so much trouble picturing the future, except in cataclysmic terms." While "(t)he cliché landmarks of tomorrow's world – vacations on the moon, robot butlers, 900 miles-per-hour transatlantic trains hurtling through vacuum tunnels – never turned up," Reynolds continues, "the absence of futuristic-ness is felt equally in the fabric of daily life, in the way that the experience of cooking an egg or taking a shower hasn't changed in our lifetime." As the twentieth century ideal of progress fades, nostalgia on the contrary is powerful and widespread.[17]

Coda

So, what comes after nostalgia, then?

Some might say that punk was actually right in the end. "No future" awaits us. But, does it?

If "the future is unwritten," as punk icon Joe Strummer famously said, yet in these times of crisis predictions of future societal scenarios have become a popular exercise and an emergent literary genre. James Bridle argues we are entering a New Dark Age, constituted by a frightening AI dystopia.[18] Umair Haque contends we are witnessing the rise of a new version of fascism, this time born and bred among those who defeated the first one: Americans. In another piece, the same author describes the future of work as "technofeudalism."[19] One point seems to be quite recurrent: the recognition that capitalism "as we know it" is dying. *Jacobin* writer Peter Frase envisages four possible versions of the future after capitalism: Communism – achieved by getting rid of labor; Rentism – basically, a more unequal version of capitalism; Socialism – a version of Communism blended with planning and a revisitation of the market economy; and Exterminism, essentially Communism for the rich few.[20] Paul Mason, instead, is the most prominent figure among those who believe that the left should embrace in full a "postcapitalist" vision, based on the combination of post-work politics and the decentralization processes enabled by the Internet.[21] But, let's remember where we started from: *it is easier to imagine the end of the world than the end of capitalism.*[22] The promise of democratization that characterized the Internet in its early stages is now conspicuously revealed as a delusion, as vividly shown by the Cambridge Analytica scandal, while a version of capitalism "on steroids," driven by digital technologies as instruments of mass surveillance, actually seems to be unfolding.[23]

Today, nostalgia looks as a rather unstoppable force of societal change. Its hegemonic rise as the cultural zeitgeist of the start of the twenty-first century represents the tip of a larger culture war, taking place at the core of societal values, which puts in contention some of the progressive achievements of the twentieth century. For the most part, this culture war is played out along the usual lines of conservative and progressive culture. Yet, interestingly, some of the cultural stances on certain issues have shifted considerably: take the anti-globalist positions that were the landmark proposition of the radical left movements of the late 1990s and early 2000s, which have now been taken up by the new movements of the right and restyled into a nationalist claim. Concomitantly, the struggle against political correctness, gender equality and "cultural Marxism," is perhaps a sign of how the progressive social achievements of the twentieth century are under threat precisely because they have, at least in part, actually succeeded in ameliorating the conditions of minorities and shown a snippet of life in a multicultural, progressive, *different* society. As argued by Paul Preciado, the strength of this "counterrevolution" against progress is ultimately evidence of the strength of the progressive revolution that has preceded it.[24]

Some toxic years of tension most likely await us. However, the rise of movements such as Extinction Rebellion offers fresh hope that the time has finally come to properly start building a progressive and not nostalgic vision, that is up to the challenges of this era. In the end let's not forget, as argued by Franco "Bifo" Berardi, that even in the darkest of moments, even in the most nostalgic of times in society, another horizon of possibility lies dormant in between the cracks.[25] We just need to find where it is. Good luck, folks.

Notes

[1] Wolfgang Streeck, "The return of the repressed." *New Left Review*, 2017, 104, 5-18 (p. 14).

[2] Lauren Berlant, *Cruel optimism*. Durham: Duke University Press, 2017, pp. 4-5.

[3] "British tea, jam and biscuits will be at the heart of Britain's Brexit trade plans," *The Telegraph*, 2016. Available at: https://www.telegraph.co.uk/news/2016/10/18/british-tea-jam-and-biscuits-will-be-at-the-heart-of-britains-br/ (Last accessed 24 July 2019).

[4] Carolina Bandinelli, Alessandro Gandini, "Hubs vs

networks in the creative economy: towards a 'Collaborative Individualism.'" In R. Gill, A. Pratt, T. Virani (eds), *Creative Hubs in Question*, Basingstoke: Palgrave Macmillan, pp. 89-110.

[5] See: Harold Nicolson, *The Congress of Vienna: a study in allied unity, 1812-1822.* Grove Press, 2000.

[6] See: David Weir, *Decadence and the making of modernism.* Cambridge: Univ of Massachusetts Press, 1995. On the relationship between indie and romanticism, see Wendy Fonarow, *Empire of dirt.* Middletown, CT: Wesleyan University Press, 2013, p. 29.

[7] Hartmut Rosa, *Social acceleration: a new theory of modernity.* New York: Columbia University Press, 2013, p. 11-20.

[8] ibid., pp. 221.

[9] ibid., pp. 40-41.

[10] ibid., pp. 320-22.

[11] Jean Baudrillard, *America.* London: Verso, 1986, pp. 75-7 and 107.

[12] Bob Sullivan, "50 years ago, the World's Fair promised a life of leisure. We're still waiting." BoingBoing, 2014. Available at: https://boingboing.net/2014/06/05/50-years-ago-the-worlds-fai.html (Last accessed 24 July 2019).

[13] Zygmunt Bauman, *Retrotopia.* London: Polity, 2017, p. 58.

[14] Daniel H. Wilson, *Where's my jetpack?* New York: Bloomsbury, 2018, back cover.

[15] Rebecca Jennings, "Many people still believe the moon landing was fake. But who's profiting?" Vox, 2019. Available at: https://www.vox.com/the-goods/2019/6/24/18692080/moon-landing-50th-anniversary-steph-curry-conspiracy-theory-hoax (Last accessed 24 July 2019).

[16] Lee McIntyre, *Post-truth*, Cambridge, Mass: MIT Press, 2018.

[17] Simon Reynolds, *Retromania: Pop culture's addiction to its own past.* London: Faber and Faber, 2011, p. 362-5.

[18] James Bridle, *New dark age. technology and the end of the future.* London: Verso, 2018.

[19] Umair Haque, "Is the future fascist?" *Medium*, 2019. Available at: https://eand.co/is-the-future-fascist-e0a7ee69ed71 (Last accessed 24 July 2019); Umair Haque, "Technofeudalism," *Medium*, 2018. Available at: https://eand.co/technofeudalism-5603506c63db (Last accessed 24 July 2019).

[20] Peter Frase, *Four futures: life after capitalism.* London: Verso, 2016.

[21] Paul Mason, *Postcapitalism: a guide to our future.* London: Penguin, 2016.

[22] Mark Fisher, *Capitalist realism: is there no alternative?* Zero Books: John Hunt Publishing, 2009, pp. 1-12.

[23] See: Evgeni Morozov, *The net delusion: how not to liberate the world.* London, Penguin Random House, 2011; Shoshana Zuboff, *The age of surveillance capitalism: The fight for a human future at the new frontier of power.* New York: Profile Books, 2019.

[24] Paul B. Preciado, "La rivolta tecnopatriarcale," Digital Library, 2019. Available at: http://www.kabulmagazine.com/paul-b-preciado-rivolta-epoca-tecnopatriarcale/ (Last accessed 26 July 2019).

[25] Franco "Bifo" Berardi, *Futurability: the age of impotence and the horizon of possibility.* London: Verso, 2017.

Bibliography

Anslow, L. "Robots have been about to take all the jobs for more than 200 years." *Medium*, 2016. Available at: https://timeline.com/robots-have-been-about-to-take-all-the-jobs-for-more-than-200-years-5c9c08a2f41d (Last accessed 24 July 2019).

Appadurai, A. *Modernity at large: cultural dimensions of globalization* (Vol. 1). Minneapolis: University of Minnesota Press, 1996.

Aronowitz, S., and DiFazio, W. *The jobless future: sci-tech and the dogma of work.* Minneapolis: University of Minnesota Press, 1994.

Arrighi, G. *The long twentieth century: money, power, and the origins of our times.* London: Verso, 1994.

Arvidsson, A. *Changemakers: the industrious future of the digital economy.* London: Polity, 2019.

Autor, D. "Why are there still so many jobs? The history and future of workplace automation," *Journal of Economic Perspectives*, 1961, 29(3), pp. 3-30.

Baker, K. "The future of work, a history," *POLITICO*, 2018. Available at: https://www.politico.com/magazine/story 2018/01/07/the-future-of-work-a-history-216244 (Last accessed 24 July 2019).

Bandinelli, C., and Gandini, A. "Hubs vs networks in the creative economy: towards a 'Collaborative Individualism.'" In R. Gill, A. Pratt, T. Virani (eds), *Creative hubs in question*, Basingstoke: Palgrave Macmillan, 2019, pp. 89-110.

Bastani, A. *Fully automated luxury communism.* London: Verso, 2019.

Baudrillard, Jean, *America.* London: Verso, 1986, pp. 75-7 and 107.

Bauman, Z. *Retrotopia.* London: Polity, 2017.

Bauman, Z. *Liquid modernity,* London: Wiley, 2013.

BBC. "The truth about young people and Brexit," 2018. Available at: https://www.bbc.co.uk/bbcthree/article/b8d097b0-3ad4-4dd9-aa25-af6374292de0 (Last accessed 24 July 2019).

Becker, S.O., Fetzer T. and Novy, D. "Who voted for Brexit? A comprehensive district-level analysis." *Economic Policy*, 2017, 32(92), pp. 601-50.

Belk, R.W. Richard W. Pollay, "Images of ourselves: The good life in twentieth century advertising." *Journal of Consumer Research*, 1985, 11(4), pp. 887-97.

Bell, D. "The impact of advertising", *New Leader* 6 (1957): 9-11.

Berardi, F. *Futurability: The age of impotence and the horizon of possibility*. London: Verso, 2017.

Berlant, L. *Cruel optimism*. Durham: Duke University Press, 2017.

Bonini, T. *Hipster*. Milano: Doppiozero, 2014.

Borgerson, J., Schroeder, J.E. *Designed for hi-fi living: the vinyl LP in midcentury America*. Cambridge, Mass: MIT Press, 2017.

Boym, S. *Nostalgia*, 2011. Available at: http://monumenttotransformation.org/atlas-of-transformation/html/n/nostalgia/nostalgia-svetlana-boym.html (Last accessed 24 July 2019).

Boym, S. *The future of nostalgia*. New York: Basic Books, 2008.

Bregman, R. *Utopia for realists: and how we can get there*. London: Bloomsbury Publishing, 2017.

James Bridle, *New Dark Age. Technology and the End of the Future*. London: Verso, 2018. Brynjolfsson, E., and McAfee, A. *The second machine age: work, progress, and prosperity in a time of brilliant technologies*. New York: WW Norton & Company, 2014.

Brookings, *How Millennials voted this election*, 2016. Available at: https://www.brookings.edu/blog/fixgov/2016/11/21/how-millennials-voted/ (Last accessed 24 July 2019).

Bureau of Labor Statistics, *Occupational Employment Statistics, 1960-70*, 1972. Available at: https://eric.ed.gov/?id=ED073294 (Last accessed 26 April 2019).

Business Insider, *Uber has refunded customers caught up in London terror attack*, 2017. Available at: https://www.businessinsider.com/uber-refunds-customers-surge-pricing-london-terror-attack-2017-6?IR=T (Last accessed 24 July 2019).

Cairns, J. *The myth of the age of entitlement: Millennials, austerity, and hope.* Toronto: University of Toronto Press, 2017.

CBS. *Trump on Charlottesville: "I think there's blame on both sides,"* 2017. Available at: https://www.cbsnews.com/news/trump-on-charlottesville-i-think-theres-blame-on-both-sides/ (Last accessed 12 April 2019).

Cohen, L. "A consumers' republic: the politics of mass consumption in postwar America." *Journal of Consumer Research,* 2004, 31(1), pp. 236-9.

Colby, S.L. and Jennifer M. Ortman, J. M, "The baby boom cohort in the United States: 2012 to 2060." *US Census Bureau,* 2014.

Costanza, D. "Can we please stop talking about generations as if they are a thing?" *Slate,* 2018. Available at: https://amp.slate.com/technology/2018/04/the-evidence-behind-generations-is-lacking.html (Last accessed 24 July 2019).

Coupland, D. *Generation X: tales for an accelerated culture.* New York: Macmillan, 1991.

Cross, G. *Consumed nostalgia: memory in the age of fast capitalism.* New York: Columbia University Press 2015.

Currid-Halkett, E. *The sum of small things: a theory of the aspirational class.* Princeton: Princeton University Press, 2017.

Davis, F. *Yearning for yesterday: a sociology of nostalgia.* Florence, MA: Free Press, 1996

Eckhardt G., and Bardhi, F. "New dynamics of social status and distinction," *Marketing Theory,* 2019, DOI: 1470593119856650.

Eurostat. *Unemployment statistics,* 2019. Available at: https://ec.europa.eu/eurostat/statistics-explained/index.php/Unemployment_statistics#Longer-term_unemployment_trends (Last accessed 24 July 2019).

Fisher, M. *Capitalist realism: is there no alternative?* Zero Books: John Hunt Publishing, 2009. Fonarow, W. *Empire of dirt.* Middletown, CT: Wesleyan University Press, 2013, p. 29.

France, A. and Roberts, S. "The problem of social generations:

a critique of the new emerging orthodoxy in youth studies." *Journal of Youth Studies*, 2015, 18(2), pp. 215-30.

Frase, P. *Four futures: life after capitalism*. London: Verso, 2016.

Frayne, D. *The refusal of work*. London: Zed Books, 2015.

Frey, C.B., and Osborne, M. *Technology at work*. The Future of Innovation and Employment. Citi GPS: Global Perspectives & Solutionsm, 2015.

Friedman, S., Savage, M., Hanquinet, L., and Miles, A. "Cultural sociology and new forms of distinction." *Poetics*, 2015, 53, pp. 1-8.

Friedman, T.L. *Thank you for being late: an optimist's guide to thriving in the age of accelerations*. New York: Picador, 2017.

Gandini, A. "Labour process theory and the gig economy." *Human Relations*, 2019, 72(6), pp. 1039-1056.

Garrett, D. "How ad men invented the future," *Medium*, 2018. Available at: https://howwegettonext.com/how-ad-men-invented-the-future-cf3f81139c08 (Last accessed 24 July 2019).

Gauntlett, D. *Making is connecting*. London: Wiley, 2013.

Goodwin M., and Milazzo, C. "Taking back control? Investigating the role of immigration in the 2016 vote for Brexit." *The British Journal of Politics and International Relations*, 2017, 19(3), pp. 450-64.

GOV.UK, *Demographic, diversity and socioeconomic profile of Havering's population*, 2014. Available at: https://www3.havering. gov.uk/Documents/Equality-and-Diversity/Appendix%202_ Demographic,%20Diversity%20and%20Socio-economic%20 Profile%20of%20Havering's%20Population%20Jan-13.pdf (Last accessed 12 April 2019).

Graeber, D. *Bullshit jobs*. New York: Simon & Schuster, 2018.

Graham, M., Shaw, J. *Towards a fairer gig economy*. London: Meatspace Press, 2017.

Grief, M. "The hipster in the mirror," *New York Times*, 2010. Available at: http://pages.vassar.edu/fren380/files/2013/03/ The-Sociology-of-the-Hipster-Essay-NYTimes.pdf (Last accessed 24 July 2019).

Grief, M. "What was the hipster," *New York Magazine*, 2010. Available at: http://nymag.com/news/features/69129/ (Last accessed 24 July 2019).

Guardian, *The slow-burning hatred that led Thomas Mair to murder Jo Cox*, 2016. Available at: https://www.theguardian.com/uk-news/2016/nov/23/thomas-mair-slow-burning-hatred-led-to-jo-cox-murder (Last accessed 12 April 2019).

Guardian, "Horrible spike" in hate crime linked to Brexit vote, Met police say, 2017. Available at: https://www.theguardian.com/society/2016/sep/28/hate-crime-horrible-spike-brexit-vote-metropolitan-police (Last accessed 12 April 2019).

Guess, A., Nagler J., and Tucker, J. "Less than you think: prevalence and predictors of fake news dissemination on Facebook." *Science advances*, 5(1), 2019. Available at: https://advances.sciencemag.org/content/5/1/eaau4586 (Last accessed 1 July 2019).

Hall, S. "The great moving right show." *Marxism Today*, 1979, 23(1), pp. 14-20.

Harris, J. "If you've got money, you vote in...if you haven't got money, you vote out," *Guardian*, 2016. Available at: https://www.theguardian.com/politics/commentisfree/2016/jun/24/divided-britain-brexit-money-class-inequality-westminster (Last accessed 26 April 2019).

Haque, U. "Is the Future Fascist?" *Medium*, 2019. Available at: https://eand.co/is-the-future-fascist-e0a7ee69ed71 (Last accessed 24 July 2019).

Haque, U. "Technofeudalism", *Medium*, 2018. Available at: https://eand.co/technofeudalism-5603506c63db (Last accessed 24 July 2019).

Harvey, D. *A brief history of neoliberalism.* New York: Oxford University Press, 2007.

Heimann, J. *All-American ads 60s.* Taschen, 2003.

Hobsbawm, E. J. "The machine breakers," *Past & Present* 1, 1952, pp. 57-70.

Hoos, I.R. "When the computer takes over the office." In: D. Preece, I. McLoughlin, P. Dawson, *Technology, organisations and innovations: the early debates*, London: Routledge, 2000, 179-97.

Huffington Post Italia, *SWG-Analisi dei flussi di voto*, 2019. Available at: https://www.huffingtonpost.it/entry/la-lega-prosciuga-di-maio_it_5cec045de4b00356fc25b556?1az=&utm_hp_ref=it-homepage#gallery/5cec092fe4b0512156f5d298/14 (Last accessed 24 July 2019).

Jameson, F. *Postmodernism, or, the cultural logic of late capitalism*. Durham, NC: Duke University Press, 1991.

Jennings, R. "Many people still believe the moon landing was fake. But who's profiting?" *Vox*, 2019. Available at: https://www.vox.com/the-goods/2019/6/24/18692080/moon-landing-50th-anniversary-steph-curry-conspiracy-theory-hoax (Last accessed 24 July 2019).

Kendzior, S. *The view from flyover country: dispatches from the forgotten America*. New York: Flatiron Books, 2018.

Krause, M. "What is Zeitgeist? Examining period-specific cultural patterns." *Poetics*, 2019, [online], available at: https://doi.org/10.1016/j.poetic.2019.02.003.

Land, C. "Back to the future: reimagining work through craft," *Futures of Work*, 2018. Available at: https://futuresofwork.co.uk/2018/11/19/back-to-the-future-re-imagining-work-through-craft/ (Last accessed 24 July 2019).

Lasch, C. *The culture of narcissism: American life in an age of diminishing expectations*. W.W. Norton & Company, 1991.

Maciel, A.F., and Wallendorf, M. "Taste engineering: an extended consumer model of cultural competence constitution." *Journal of Consumer Research*, 2016, 43-5, 726-46.

Mailer, N. *Advertisements for myself*. Cambridge, Mass: Harvard University Press, 1959.

Marchand, R. *Advertising the American dream: making way for mo-*

dernity, 1920-1940. University of California Press, 1985.

Marglin S.A., and Schor, J.B. (Eds.). *The golden age of capitalism: reinterpreting the postwar experience.* New York: Oxford University Press, 1990.

Mason, P. *Postcapitalism: A guide to our future.* London: Penguin, 2016.

McIntyre, L. *Post-truth,* Cambridge, Mass: MIT Press, 2018.

McKinsey. *Five lessons from history on AI, automation, and employment,* 2017. Available at: https://www.mckinsey.com/featured-insights/future-of-work/five-lessons-from-history-on-ai-automation-and-employment (Last accessed 24 July 2019).

Morin, E. *L'esprit du temps.* Paris, Grasset, 1962.

Morozov, E. *The net delusion: how not to liberate the world.* London, Penguin Random House, 2011.

Nagle, A. *Kill all normies: online culture wars from 4chan and Tumblr to Trump and the alt-right.* Zero Books: John Hunt Publishing, 2017.

Nicolson, H. *The Congress of Vienna: a study in allied unity, 1812-1822.* Grove Press, 2000.

O'Connor, S. "When your boss is an algorithm," *Financial Times,* 8 September 2016.

Ocejo, R.E. *Masters of craft: old jobs in the new urban economy.* Princeton, NY: Princeton University Press, 2017.

OECD. *Under pressure: the squeezed middle class,* 2019. Available at: http://www.oecd.org/unitedstates/Middle-class-2019-United-States.pdf (Last accessed 24 July 2019).

OECD. *Data on the future of work,* 2015. Available at: https://www.oecd.org/els/emp/future-of-work/data/ (Last accessed 24 July 2019).

Ownby, T. *American dreams in Mississippi: consumers, poverty, & culture, 1830-1998.* University of North Carolina Press, 1999.

Owram, D. *Born at the right time: a history of the baby-boom generation.* Toronto: University of Toronto Press, 1997.

Palahniuk, C. *Fight Club: a novel*. W.W. Norton & Company, 2005.

Pew Research Centre. *Millennial life. How young adulthood today compares with prior generations*, 2019 Available at: https://www. pewsocialtrends.org/essay/millennial-life-how-young-adulthood-today-compares-with-prior-generations/ (Last accessed 24 July 2019).

Pew Research Centre. *Millennials approach Baby Boomers as America's largest generation in the electorate*, 2018. Available at: https://www.pewresearch.org/fact-tank/2018/04/03/millennials-approach-baby-boomers-as-largest-generation-in-u-s-electorate/ (Last accessed 24 July 2019).

Pew Research Centre. *Religion among the Millennials*, 2010. Available at: https://www.pewforum.org/2010/02/17/religion-among-the-millennials/ (Last accessed 24 July 2019).

Pink, D.H. *Free agent nation: How America's new independent workers are transforming the way we live*. Business Plus, 2001.

POLITICO, *Full transcript: Donald Trump's jobs plan speech*, 2016. Available at: https://www.politico.com/story/2016/06/full-transcript-trump-job-plan-speech-224891 (Last accessed 26 April 2019).

Preciado, P.B. "La rivolta tecnopatriarcale," Digital Library, 2019. Available at: http://www.kabulmagazine.com/paul-b-preciado-rivolta-epoca-tecnopatriarcale/ (Last accessed 26 July 2019).

Putnam, R.D. *Our kids: the American dream in crisis*. New York: Simon and Schuster, 2016.

Reeve, E. "This is what the life of an incel looks like," *Vice Magazine*, 2017. Available from: https://news.vice.com/en_us/article/7xqw3g/this-is-what-the-life-of-an-incel-looks-like?utm_source=vicefbus (Last accessed 22 July 2019).

Reynolds, S. *Retromania: pop culture's addiction to its own past*. London: Faber and Faber, 2011.

Jeremy Rifkin, *The end of work*. New York: Putnam, 1995.

Rosa, H. "Dynamic stabilization, the Triple A. Approach to the good life, and the resonance conception," Questions de communication, 2017, (1), pp. 437-56.

Rosa, H. *Social acceleration: a new theory of modernity.* New York: Columbia University Press, 2013.

Schiermer, B. Late-modern hipsters: new tendencies in popular culture. *Acta Sociologica*, 2014, 57(2), pp. 167-81.

Schinco, E. "Amara Terra Mia – L'emigrazione italiana," *Senso Comune*, 2017. Available at: https://www.senso-comune.it/rivista/penisola/amara-terra-mia-lemigrazione-italiana/ (Last accessed 24 July 2019).

Sennett, R. *The Craftsman.* New Haven: Yale University Press, 2008.

Srnicek N., and Williams, A. *Inventing the future: postcapitalism and a world without work.* London: Verso, 2015.

Stein, J. "Millennials: The me me me generation," *Time*, 2013. Available at: https://time.com/247/millennials-the-me-me-me-generation/ (Last accessed 24 July2019).

Streeck, W. "The return of the repressed." *New Left Review*, 2017, 104, pp. 5-18.

The Atlantic, *Read: Obama's Speech on the Middle Class*, 2013. Available at: https://www.theatlantic.com/politics/archive/2013/07/read-obamas-speech-middle-class/312948/ (Last accessed 26 April 2019).

Sullivan, B. "50 years ago, the World's Fair promised a life of leisure. We're still waiting." *BoingBoing*, 2014. Available at: https://boingboing.net/2014/06/05/50-years-ago-the-worlds-fai.html (Last accessed 24 July 2019).

The Economist. *The world is fixated on the past*, 2018. Available at: https://www.economist.com/leaders/2018/12/22/the-world-is-fixated-on-the-past (Last accessed 12 April 2019).

The Economist. *Workers on tap*, 2014. Available at: https://www.economist.com/leaders/2014/12/30/workers-on-tap (Last accessed 24 July 2019).

The Independent. *UK weather: Deliveroo faces criticism over driv-*

er safety in heavy snow, 2018. Available at: https://www.independent.co.uk/life-style/food-and-drink/deliveroo-driver-safety-uk-weather-snow-criticism-extra-charge-delivery-a8236966.html (Last accessed 24 July 2019).

The Telegraph. *British tea, jam and biscuits will be at the heart of Britain's Brexit trade plans,* 2016. Available at: https://www.telegraph.co.uk/news/2016/10/18/british-tea-jam-and-biscuits-will-be-at-the-heart-of-britains-br/ (Last accessed 24 July 2019).

Thompson, P. "The Refusal of Work: Past, Present and Future," *Futures of Work,* 2018. Available at: https://futuresofwork.co.uk/2018/09/05/the-refusal-of-work-past-present-and-future/ https://futuresofwork.co.uk/2018/09/05/editorial-from-the-future-of-work-to-futures-of-work/ (Last accessed 24 July 2019).

Time, "Living: proceeding with caution," 2019. Available at: http://content.time.com/time/subscriber/article/0,33009,970634-1,00.html (Last accessed 26 April 2019).

Vallas, S.P. "Platform capitalism: what's at stake for workers?" *New Labor Forum,* 2018, 28 (1), pp. 48-59.

Weir, D. *Decadence and the making of modernism.* Cambridge: University of Massachusetts Press, 1995.

Welsh, I. *Trainspotting.* Sekcer and Warburg, 1993.

Westacott, E. "What does it mean to live the 'good life'?", 2019. Available at: https://www.thoughtco.com/what-is-the-good-life-4038226 (last accessed 12 April 2019).

Williams A., and Srnicek, N. *#ACCELERATE MANIFESTO for an Accelerationist Politics,* 2013. Available at: http://criticallegalthinking.com/2013/05/14/accelerate-manifesto-for-an-accelerationist-politics/ (Last accessed 24 July 2019).

Williams, J. C. *White working class: Overcoming class cluelessness in America.* Cambridge, Mass: Harvard Business Press, 2017.

Wilson, D.H. *Where's my jetpack?.* New York: Bloomsbury, 2018.

Wilson, J. "Gen X has survived its gloomy years. Now we will have to deal with climate change," *Guardian*, 2019. Available at: https://www.theguardian.com/environment/commentis-free/2019/feb/21/gen-x-has-survived-its-gloomy-formative-years-now-we-will-have-to-deal-with-climate-change (Last accessed 24 July 2019)

Wilson, J.L. *Nostalgia: sanctuary of meaning.* Lewisburg, PA: Bucknell University Press, 2005.

Wolfe, T. "The 'Me' Decade and the Third Great Awakening." *New York Magazine,* 1976. Available at: http://nymag.com/news/features/45938/ (Last accessed 26 April 2019).

Wright Mills, C. *White collar; the American middle classes,* New York, 1951, pp. 324-54.

Zuboff, S. *The age of surveillance capitalism: the fight for a human future at the new frontier of power.* New York: Profile Books, 2019.

Zukin, S. "Consuming authenticity: from outposts of difference to means of exclusion". *Cultural studies,* 2008, 22(5), pp. 724-48.

CULTURE, SOCIETY & POLITICS

The modern world is at an impasse. Disasters scroll across our smartphone screens and we're invited to like, follow or upvote, but critical thinking is harder and harder to find. Rather than connecting us in common struggle and debate, the internet has sped up and deepened a long-standing process of alienation and atomization. Zer0 Books wants to work against this trend. With critical theory as our jumping off point, we aim to publish books that make our readers uncomfortable. We want to move beyond received opinions.

Zer0 Books is on the left and wants to reinvent the left. We are sick of the injustice, the suffering and the stupidity that defines both our political and cultural world, and we aim to find a new foundation for a new struggle.

If this book has helped you to clarify an idea, solve a problem or extend your knowledge, you may want to check out our online content as well. Look for Zer0 Books: Advancing Conversations in the iTunes directory and for our Zer0 Books YouTube channel.

Popular videos include:

Žižek and the Double Blackmain

The Intellectual Dark Web is a Bad Sign

Can there be an Anti-SJW Left?

Answering Jordan Peterson on Marxism

Follow us on Facebook
at https://www.facebook.com/ZeroBooks and Twitter at https://twitter.com/Zer0Books

Bestsellers from Zer0 Books include:

Give Them An Argument
Logic for the Left
Ben Burgis
Many serious leftists have learned to distrust talk of logic. This is a serious mistake.
Paperback: 978-1-78904-210-8 ebook: 978-1-78904-211-5

Poor but Sexy
Culture Clashes in Europe East and West
Agata Pyzik
How the East stayed East and the West stayed West.
Paperback: 978-1-78099-394-2 ebook: 978-1-78099-395-9

An Anthropology of Nothing in Particular
Martin Demant Frederiksen
A journey into the social lives of meaninglessness.
Paperback: 978-1-78535-699-5 ebook: 978-1-78535-700-8

In the Dust of This Planet
Horror of Philosophy vol. 1
Eugene Thacker
In the first of a series of three books on the Horror of Philosophy,
In the Dust of This Planet offers the genre of horror as a way of
thinking about the unthinkable.
Paperback: 978-1-84694-676-9 ebook: 978-1-78099-010-1

The End of Oulipo?
An Attempt to Exhaust a Movement
Lauren Elkin, Veronica Esposito
Paperback: 978-1-78099-655-4 ebook: 978-1-78099-656-1

Capitalist Realism
Is There no Alternative?
Mark Fisher
An analysis of the ways in which capitalism has presented itself
as the only realistic political-economic system.
Paperback: 978-1-84694-317-1 ebook: 978-1-78099-734-6

Rebel Rebel
Chris O'Leary
David Bowie: every single song. Everything you want to know,
everything you didn't know.
Paperback: 978-1-78099-244-0 ebook: 978-1-78099-713-1

Kill All Normies
Angela Nagle
Online culture wars from 4chan and Tumblr to Trump.
Paperback: 978-1- 78535-543-1 ebook: 978-1-78535-544-8

Cartographies of the Absolute
Alberto Toscano, Jeff Kinkle
An aesthetics of the economy for the twenty-first century.
Paperback: 978-1-78099-275-4 ebook: 978-1-78279-973-3

Malign Velocities
Accelerationism and Capitalism
Benjamin Noys
Long listed for the Bread and Roses Prize 2015, *Malign Velocities*
argues against the need for speed, tracking acceleration
as the symptom of the ongoing crises of capitalism.
Paperback: 978-1-78279-300-7 ebook: 978-1-78279-299-4

Meat Market
Female Flesh under Capitalism
Laurie Penny
A feminist dissection of women's bodies as the fleshy fulcrum of
capitalist cannibalism, whereby women are both consumers and
consumed.
Paperback: 978-1-84694-521-2 ebook: 978-1-84694-782-7

Babbling Corpse
Vaporwave and the Commodification of Ghosts
Grafton Tanner
Paperback: 978-1-78279-759-3 ebook: 978-1-78279-760-9

New Work New Culture
Work we want and a culture that strengthens us
Frithjoff Bergmann
A serious alternative for mankind and the planet.
Paperback: 978-1-78904-064-7 ebook: 978-1-78904-065-4

Enjoying It
Candy Crush and Capitalism
Alfie Bown
A study of enjoyment and of the enjoyment of studying. Bown asks what enjoyment says about us and what we say about enjoyment, and why.
Paperback: 978-1-78535-155-6 ebook: 978-1-78535-156-3

Color, Facture, Art and Design
Iona Singh
This materialist definition of fine-art develops guidelines for architecture, design, cultural-studies and ultimately social change.
Paperback: 978-1-78099-629-5 ebook: 978-1-78099-630-1

Neglected or Misunderstood
The Radical Feminism of Shulamith Firestone
Victoria Margree
An interrogation of issues surrounding gender, biology, sexuality, work and technology, and the ways in which our imaginations continue to be in thrall to ideologies of maternity and the nuclear family.
Paperback: 978-1-78535-539-4 ebook: 978-1-78535-540-0

How to Dismantle the NHS in 10 Easy Steps (Second Edition)
Youssef El-Gingihy
The story of how your NHS was sold off and why you will have to buy private health insurance soon. A new expanded second edition with chapters on junior doctors' strikes and government blueprints for US-style healthcare.
Paperback: 978-1-78904-178-1 ebook: 978-1-78904-179-8

Digesting Recipes
The Art of Culinary Notation
Susannah Worth
A recipe is an instruction, the imperative tone of the expert, but this constraint can offer its own kind of potential. A recipe need not be a domestic trap but might instead offer escape – something to fantasise about or aspire to.
Paperback: 978-1-78279-860-6 ebook: 978-1-78279-859-0

Most titles are published in paperback and as an ebook. Paperbacks are available in traditional bookshops. Both print and ebook formats are available online.
Follow us on Facebook
at https://www.facebook.com/ZeroBooks
and Twitter at https://twitter.com/Zer0Books